THE
BEGINNING
OF
CHINESE
CHARACTERS

THE BEGINNING OF CHINESE CHARACTERS

Ethel R. Nelson,
Richard E. Broadberry,
Samuel Wang

Read Books Publisher
Dunlap, TN

All Scriptures quoted, unless otherwise specified, are from the Holy Bible, New King James Version, copyright © 1982, Thomas Nelson, Inc. Used by permission.

Copyright © 2001 Ethel R. Nelson

Published by Read Books Publisher
HCR 65 Box 580
Dunlap, TN 37327, USA

All rights reserved. No part of this publication may be reproduced, stored in a retrieval system, or transmitted, in any form or by any means, electronic, mechanical, photocopying, recording, or otherwise, without the prior written permission of the author.

ISBN 0-937869-03-1

Library of Congress Catalog Number 00 091715

Dedication

To J. B. Talovitch, whom I have never met,...

but who played a major role in piquing my interest in ancient Chinese characters. After the publication of *Discovery of Genesis* (Concordia, 1979), I received a letter from this gentleman, whom I learned was a Chinese philologist. He suggested that analysis of characters could only be legitimate if confirmed by more ancient forms. From Dr. Talovitch, I obtained my first books with bronzeware graphs. These fascinating pictograms immediately initiated more in-depth study—and discovery!

Ethel R. Nelson, M.D.

CONTENTS

An Introduction to the Radical Study****** ix

Sections

I Beginnings—God............................ 17

"I am the Alpha and the Omega, the Beginning and the End, says the Lord, "who is and who was and who is to come, the Almighty."

(Revelation 1: 8)

II Beginnings—Creation...................... 55

[Jesus said] "From the beginning of the creation, God 'made them male and female.'"

(Mark 10: 6).

III Beginnings—Worship of God......... 101

*A glorious high throne from
   the beginning
Is the place of our Sanctuary.*

(Jeremiah 17: 12).

IV Beginnings—Sin.......................... 133

He [the devil] was a murderer from the beginning, and does not stand in the truth, because there is no truth in him...for he is a liar and the father of it.
(John 8: 44).

V Beginnings—Salvation................... 153

... God from the beginning chose you for salvation through sanctification by the Spirit and belief in the truth.
(2 Thessalonians 2: 13)

VI Beginnings—Garden of Eden Topography.............. 183

*Great is the LORD, and Greatly to be praised
In the city of our God, in His holy mountain.
Beautiful in elevation, the joy of the whole earth,
Is Mount Zion on the sides of the north....
Walk about Zion, and go all around her.
Count her towers;...*
(Psalm 48: 1,2,12).

Appendices
    A. "My Holy Hill............................ 235
    B. Significance of the Sanctuary   245

Bibliography.. 251

Radical Index... 253

AN INTRODUCTION TO THE RADICAL STUDY

Whereas the Western world, for the most part, uses a 26-letter alphabet to form words in the scores of languages represented, the Chinese have a more unique system. Today's Chinese "alphabet" consists of 214 "radicals" used to form the traditional characters, or 226 to write the simplified characters. However, 2,000 years ago, the Chinese "alphabet" consisted of 540 "radicals!" Exactly what are these symbols? The original Chinese radicals were simple pictographs, some with meanings which allowed them to stand alone, while others needed to be combined with other radicals to form meaningful concepts, called "ideographs."

Obviously, the radicals (also called "keys," "elements," or "primitives") are the fundamental building blocks of the written Chinese language, and consequently the most ancient "elements" of the writing. The oldest writing has been found on the so-called "oracle bones" used for divination. The bronzeware characters (inscribed on the inner lips of ancient bronze vessels) date as far back as the second dynasty, the Shang (1766 B.C.). The next artistic form was the seal writing (also called the *Shuo Wen*), used for several centuries until today's "traditional" script took over about 2,000 years ago. So one can see an evolution of the calligraphy, but somehow, miraculously, their basic meanings, although today sometimes obsolete, have remained intact.

The origin of ancient Chinese writing has always been enshrouded in mystery. Who really invented these symbols? How old are they? Do the characters have more than a superficial meaning? And above all, why has this ancient, cumbersome writing survived into our technological 21st century so dedicated to speed and user-friendliness? Is character-analysis legitimate?

Because fortune tellers have for centuries used Chinese characters in a magical sense, known as "chezi" (折字), some serious Chinese scholars may justifiably have questions initially regarding any analysis of characters. Such fortune-telling use of the characters may trace roots back even to the second century. During the Sui Dynasty (589-618 A.D.), this analysis was called "pozi" (破字), while it was known as "xiangzi" (相字)in the Song Dynasty (960-1279 A.D.) Even today this practice is still popular in some Chinese circles. Those performing such "magic," draw one or several characters, and after adding or subtracting various radicals, determine one's future by analyzing the remaining components composing the characters.

This divination practice, however, need not cast suspicion on all our work of many years. While Satan, the prince of darkness and deception, has endeavored to bring a disreputable shadow and doubt to all forms of character-analysis, the light shining from the Holy Bible will bring out the true meanings buried in the ancient Chinese radicals. Fractional glimpses of the life and faith of the ancient Chinese people will be brought into view. The consistency of Truth will speak for itself.

In light of the incredible similarities between the original religion of the Chinese and that of the Hebrews, it seems plausible to us, and also to others, that the Chinese written language, might be a hieroglyphic system [sacred, yet plain, writing]. In fact from our 25 years of research, we are awed and fully persuaded that the foundation of the Chinese characters draws from the same Source as the early chapters of Genesis, the first book of the Hebrew Bible. *"That was the true Light which gives light to every man who comes into the world." (John1:9)*.

The Chinese people have greatly reverenced their historical past and are proud that they are a people with over 4,000 years of continuous existence. Much information can be gathered from a study of their ancient classical writings that have been miraculously preserved over the millennia. From these writings, fragmentary history can be learned, but most important, an understanding of their religious focus.[1] Surprisingly, perhaps, is the fact that the ancients earnestly worshiped their Creator-God, *Tian* [Heaven, God], also known as *ShangDi* [the Heavenly Ruler]. Note this recitation from their 4,000 year-old annual Border Sacrifice:

When Te [ShangDi], the Lord, had so decreed, He called into existence [created] heaven, earth, and man.[2]

Another ancient people, the Hebrews, also recorded for all time their history, dating back to the creation of the world. This 3,500 year-old chronicle, written over a span of 1,600 years by about 40 different authors, under the inspiration of their God, was eventually drawn together and preserved unscathed for millennia. It is the only document that narrates earth's and mankind's beginnings in detail. It is a sacred document, treasured as absolute truth by a large portion of earth's inhabitants today. It is a book which, although chronicling the pre-Hebrew history, nevertheless should be of great interest to the Chinese as well as all mankind. In a remarkable way, the Chinese characters relate exactly the same historical features, which testify to the validity of both the Hebrew and Chinese writings. These Scriptures, for the past several centuries, have been collected into what is known as the Holy Bible.

Amazing as it may seem, we have found that the Chinese God [Tian, ShangDi] is a Creator-God identical to the Hebrew God.[3] Furthermore, the Chinese God, like that of the Hebrews, is actually a "Godhead" [Trinity] of three separate Persons who act as one.[4] By the ancient Chinese, their Godhead was known as "Dao" [Tao]. Note how Lao Zi (c. 570 B.C.) referred to this mysterious, omnipotent, omniscient, omnipresent God:

> **Look, it cannot be seen—it is beyond form.**
> **Listen, it cannot be heard—it is beyond sound.**
> **Grasp, it cannot be held—it is intangible.**
> **These three are indefinable;**
> **Therefore they are joined in one. . . .**
> **Stay with the ancient Dao**
> **Move with the present**
> <u>**Knowing the ancient beginning is the**</u>
> <u>**essence of Dao**</u>.[5]
>
> **The Dao exists as one.**
> **One exists as two.**
> **Two exist as three.**
> **And three create everything.**[6]

Compare this with the Bible:

> *For there are three who bear witness in heaven:*
> *the Father, the Word [Jesus Christ], and the Holy*
> *Spirit; and these three are one, (1 John 5: 7).*

This Godhead, revealed in the Chinese ancient writings, is identical to the Creator-God of the ancient Hebrew people as found in the sacred Hebrew writings, today preserved in the Holy Bible.

But how did the Chinese people come to occupy China in the first place? According to Biblical chronology, about 100 years after the universal flood in the time of Noah, some of his descendants again entertained a rebellious spirit against God. They determined to build a city and tower. God intervened, causing a great division of peoples and confusion of language:

> *[the LORD said. . .]. "Come, let Us go down and there*
> *confuse their language, that they may not understand one*
> *another's speech." So the LORD scattered them abroad from there*

over the face of all the earth, and they ceased building the city.
(Genesis 11: 7, 8).

According to the Biblical chronology, studied out by James Ussher (1586-1656) an Irish archbishop of Armagh, this Babel incident occurred about the year 2247 B.C. It is noteworthy that the first Chinese dynasty, the Xia, was founded in 2205 B.C., allowing time, following the division of peoples, for migration and settlement of the first Chinese. Evidently the Chinese family did not participate in the rebellion. Wrote the ancient Chinese:

> **The great Tian [Heaven, God] gave**
> **this Middle Kingdom [ancient**
> **China] with its people and**
> **territories to the former kings.**[7]

Not only did they record that the God of Heaven established their Chinese civilization, but that God gave it to their "former kings." We learn further that these early kings were righteous rulers. The venerable teachers, such as Confucius, Lao Zi and Mencius,[8] were also righteous men Again they documented that

> **Tian [Heaven] gives birth to kings;**
> **Heaven gives birth to teachers.**
> **The kings and teachers are assistants**
> **of Heaven to teach the people the love of Heaven.**[9]

Is it any wonder then that not only their ancient record-writing, but also their character-writing have a sacred orientation? In fact, even the basic pictographic radicals themselves retell the Genesis stories of the creation, worship of the man and woman in the Garden of Eden, the temptation and fall into sin of the first human couple, and God's solution for the sin problem. The actual topography of Eden is also given. But these stories as recorded in the characters have been lost sight of through the intervening 4,000 years since the invention of the writing.

In 86 B.C., Hsu Shen, a Chinese scholar, finished his monumental work—the *Shuo Wen,* actually, the first Chinese dictionary—that was finally published posthumously.[10] He attempted, approximately 2,000 years after the invention of the writing, to analyze the meanings of the characters. His work has survived another 2,000 years and today still forms the basis for most scholarly studies into the language. However, Hsu Shen was far removed from the culture of the ancients, and by his day, religious concepts had blurred and become distorted. Mystical or philosophical interpretations had been given to the writings of Lao Zi (c.570 B.C) and Confucius(551-479.B.C.), borrowing from, but distorting much of the original spiritual concepts. However, the characters inscribed on the oracle bones and bronzeware vessels remain a reliable source to trace some of the original thought.

This present work is not exactly a dictionary, as was Hsu Shen's book, but a commentary. We have departed from the traditional stroke-numbering categorizing of the more than 200 radicals, and have endeavored instead to arrange these "key" pictograms, not only chronologically, but also logically. In so doing, they tell a story of earth's beginnings and follow, very closely, the only complete history of origins as related by the Hebrew Scriptures [Holy Bible]. Since Lao Zi (above) advised that "**Knowing the ancient beginning is the essence of Dao,**" we have divided this book according to the various "Beginnings" of earth and of human history. We will naturally begin with God, His specific attributes, and a discussion of the various names of God.

In this present work, undertaking the analysis of the most primitive elements of the writing, the 214 "traditional" radicals have been examined. In addition, five radicals from the "simplified" radical list have been included, making a total of 219 radicals studied. At the completion of the study, we found that of these 219 key characters, 184 were related to their original knowledge of God and events taking place in the Garden of Eden or at its gate. Since the radicals are the most primitive elements of the Chinese writing and

84% of them have sacred relevance, it would surely seem that a divine theme is the whole basis of this ancient writing. One has solid grounds to believe that the Chinese writing is truly a hieroglyphic language!

An additional explanation should be made concerning Section VI, which discusses the possible topography of the Garden of Eden in the light of the Bible and ancient Chinese pictographic radicals. The commentary regarding the Holy Mountain of Eden and the heavenly New Jerusalem is a subject that I have personally researched historically and Biblically, and have pondered and prayed over for more than 20 years. Admittedly, there are many Bible mysteries, of which the details of Eden is doubtless one. I would trust our readers' good judgment to prayerfully compare what I have presented in this section with the Bible and historical documents. You may agree and even appreciate that which I believe is hidden in the ancient Chinese graphs. You are also free to disagree!

We are deeply indebted to two Christian artists who use the Chinese characters in their languages, Mr. Li Weishan, a Chinese; and Mr. Shunichi Yamamoto, a Japanese. Mr. Li painted the cover and Mr. Yamamoto drew and painted the internal illustrations. Their artistry contributes to the clarity of the presentation.

As the radicals are presented, the first number represents the "traditional" index listing, while the number of the "simplified" follows in the parenthesis, according to its numerical index.

Ethel R. Nelson, M.D.
Dunlap, Tennessee
October 1, 2000

1. Samuel Wang and Ethel R. Nelson, *God and the Ancient Chinese* (Dunlap, TN: Read Books Publ., 1999).

2. James Legge, *The Notions of the Chinese Concerning God and Spirits* (Hong Kong: Hong Kong Register, 1852), p. 29.

3. Ethel R. Nelson, Richard Broadberry and Ginger Chock, *God's Promise to the Chinese* (Dunlap, TN: Read Books Publ., 1997), pp. 7-14.

4. Op. cit. Wang and Nelson, *God and the Ancient Chinese*, pp. 47-71.

5. Gia Fu Feng and Jane English, *Translation of Lao Zi: Tao Te Ching* (Toronto: Vintage Books, Random House, Inc. 1989), Chap 14, p. 16. See also Ibid. Wang and Nelson, p. 67.

6. Ibid. Chap 42, p. 44. (Retranslated by Samuel Wang). See also Wang and Nelson, p. 70.

7. James legge, *The Chinese Classics, Vol. III, The Shu Jing* (Taipei: SMC Publ. Inc. 1983), Part V, Bk. XI, Para. 6, p. 418.

8. Op. cit. Wang and Nelson, pp. 10-16.

9. Op. cit. James Legge, *The Shu Jing,* Part V, Bk. I, Part 7, p. 286..

10. G.D.Wilder and J.H. Ingram, *Analysis of Chinese Characters,* (Taipei: Chin Wen Publ. Co., 1964), p. vi.

Section I

BEGINNINGS—GOD

" I am the Alpha and the Omega, the Beginning and the End," says the Lord, "who is and who was and who is to come, the Almighty."
(Revelation 1: 8)

In the Beginning—God

𝕬s we begin this study of the 4,000-year-old Chinese radicals (using the oracle bone, bronzeware, and seal graphs), a comparison with the Holy Bible is most helpful historically. Selected Chinese radicals beautifully portray their Creator-God—actually, the Godhead of three distinct Divine Beings. It is amazing to see how closely the Chinese pictograms follow the same characteristics of God as depicted in the Bible.

The first book and chapter of the Scriptures is called GENESIS, meaning "The Beginning." In Sections I and II, we will deal with the ancient radicals that describe the Creator-God beginning His activity of forming our earth and its contents in six, literal, 24-hour days. In this present Section, the divine attributes of the Godhead will be detailed.

A few relevant verses from another ancient inspired Biblical author, JOB, follow. These quotations are an illustrative introduction to the all-knowing, all-powerful, all-wise God whom the Chinese radicals have so-well captured in their expressive pictograms!

Genesis 1: 1-10

> *In the beginning God created the heavens and the earth.*
> *The earth was without form, and void; and darkness was on*

the face of the deep. And the Spirit of God was hovering over the face of the waters.

Then God said, "Let there be light"; and there was light.

And God saw the light, that it was good; and God divided the light from the darkness.

God called the light Day, and the darkness He called Night. So the evening and the morning were the first day.

Then God said, "Let there be a firmament [expanse] in the midst of the waters, and let it divide the waters from the waters." Thus God made the firmament, and divided the waters which were under the firmament from the waters which were above the firmament; and it was so.

And God called the firmament Heaven. So the evening and the morning were the second day.

Then God said, "Let the waters under the heavens be gathered together into one place, and let the dry land appear"; and it was so. And God called the dry land Earth, and the gathering together of the waters He called Seas. And God saw that it was good.

Job 38: 4-11:

Then the LORD answered Job out of the whirlwind, and said: . . .
   "Where were you when I laid
      the foundations of the earth?
   Tell me, if you have
      understanding.
   Who determined its
      measurements?
   Surely you know!
   Or who stretched the line
      upon it?
   To what were its foundations
      fastened?
   Or who laid its cornerstone,
   When the morning stars sang
      together,

*And all the sons of God
shouted for joy?
Or who shut in the sea with
doors,
When it burst forth
and issued from the womb;
When I made the clouds its
garment,
And thick darkness its
swaddling band;
When I fixed My limit for it,
And set bars and doors;
When I said,
'This far you may come,
but no farther,
And here your proud waves
must stop!'"*

Ancient Hebrew, Greek, Egyptian hieroglyphs, Sumerian cuneiform, etc. are known and appreciated today by only a relatively few scholars. On the other hand, Chinese, an even older writing, is used by over a billion people on a daily basis. Even though the script has been modified from its early strictly pictographic forms, yet enough clues have been preserved to trace its original concepts of God as three divine Persons. The following 34 radicals convey these early beliefs in a Godhead of Three Divine Beings.

Radical 30 (58)   ∪   ∪   □   □

Oracle bone Bronzeware Traditional Simplified

Definition: mouth, person, speak, eat, breathe

Analysis: The *mouth* ∪, ▽, □, ○ (□) takes various configurations in oracle bone and bronzeware characters.

The mouth's many functions symbolize not only speaking, but also eating and breathing. The mouth becomes a person in the idiom "so many mouths to feed." Therefore, the mouth radical is possibly the most commonly-used and important of all radicals.

The original God of China, *Shangdi*, 帝¹ (上帝) the "Heavenly Ruler," was often simply referred to as *Di*. A second oracle bone version of the character *Di* is 帝 ². Note here three *mouths* ▷ + ▽ + ◁ , indicating three Persons, the Godhead (see also R. 113, p. 28). The Hebrew name for God, "Elohim," also characterizes plural divine Beings. Both the Chinese and Hebrews' concept of God was three Persons acting as One— the Trinity. How significant that the *mouth* is used to picture Shangdi, for He created all things by *speaking or breathing* them into existence, according to this recitation from the annual emperors' Border Sacrifice:

> **When Di, the Lord, had so decreed, He <u>called into existence</u> heaven and earth. He separately placed in order men and things, all overspread by the heavens.³**

The Hebrew record, the Bible, relates the same in Psalm 33: 6, 9, TEV :

> *The LORD created the heavens by His command, the sun, moon, and stars by His spoken word. . .When He spoke, the world was created; at His command everything appeared.*

Radical (90)

天 大 天 天

Oracle bone Bronzeware Traditional Simplified

Definition: *Tian,* Heaven, God, sky, day, nature

Analysis:

    great (Person)   above   Tian, Heaven, God

In the Beginning—God

Tian, Heaven, God, 天 , 大 4 (天) reveals a *great, noble* 大 (大) *Person* coming from *above* 二 (上), and is thus prophetic of Jesus Christ, the Son of God, who left heaven to live on earth and die for our sins. The second oracle bone figure, 大 presents a symbol for the head meaning *a flame of fire* ◇ , (see next R 3). This represents God's holiness, or glory. The "blackening" of the head in the bronzeware figure, *Tian, Heaven, God* 天 5 (天), has the same significance.

Said Ban Gu (班固), from the first century Han Dynasty, **"Tian [Heaven] is the supreme Guardian who sits in the most high place, ruling over everything."**6 According to the *Shuo Wen,* **"Tian [Heaven] is the greatest, is the beginning of everything, and controls everything."**7

The ancient Chinese had a deep, significant meaning of "Tian." This was the most honorable title used to address the supreme Ruler and Creator of heaven and earth. Therefore, they realized that everything belonged to Tian: nature, space, time, were created and owned by Him. For this reason, "Tian" has been used to describe all of these, and accounts also for the multiple definitions of the word, Tian (天).

Cheng Hsuan (鄭玄), a scholar of the early Han dynasty, stated, **"Shangdi** 帝 **(上帝, the *Heavenly Ruler*), is another name for Tian [Heaven.]"**8 Shun, a ruler in the "Legendary Period of Five Rulers," sacrificed to Shangdi. China's kings and emperors, for 4,000 years, annually sacrificed a bull to Shangdi at the Border Sacrifice.9

Tian 天 and Shangdi 帝 are two of several names used for the Chinese Creator-God.

Radical
3 (1)

Oracle bone Bronzeware Traditional Simplified

Definition: flame of fire
Analysis:

◊ as seen in ◊◊
flame   *fire*

This symbol ◊ (ˋ) is seen in many oracle bone characters (● in bronzeware), and usually carries the meaning of holiness or glory. It is appropriate as God's glory is described as "a flame of fire" in the Hebrew Scriptures: *"And the Angel of the LORD [God] appeared to him in a flame of fire from the midst of a bush." (Exodus 3: 2)*. Review Radical (90), p. 22, 大, *Tian, Heaven , God,* where ◊ forms God's "head." Compare the description of God the Son in Revelation 1: 14, 16: *"His eyes like a flame of fire"* and *"His countenance was like the sun shining in its strength."*

The character meaning *holy* 10 (聖) portrays God's *hands* (爪 , see R. 87, next radical) molding the *clay* (土 , see R. 32, p. 68) to form the first human, who was "made in God's image" (Genesis 1: 27) and therefore, "holy." (See Section II).

Radical 87 (116)

Oracle bone Bronzeware Traditional Simplified

Definition: hand, claw, to grasp (hand of God)
Analysis: A *hand* (爪) reaching down from above would appear to be God's hand. Note the three "fingers" which could represent, again, the creative work of the three Persons of the Godhead.

The *hand* may be found singly, as in *satisfactory, prepare* 11 (妥, see R. 38, p. 79) where God's *hand* is *preparing* the first

In the Beginning—God

woman 𠨰 (女); or in *imprint, seal.* 𠨱 12 (印, see R. 26) with God's *hand* 𠂇 *imprinting* 𠨱 His character (image) upon the first man 𠂊 (卩). Both *hands* 𠬞 of God may be found, in *holy* 𡆣 (聖 , see discussion under R. 32, p. 68).

Radical 24 (12)

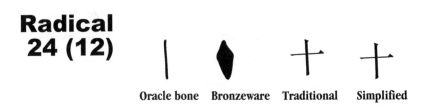

Oracle bone   Bronzeware   Traditional   Simplified

Definition: complete, perfect, ten

Analysis: We believe this simple stroke in the oracle bone carries the meaning of a *complete, perfect* | 13 (十) person, either a human, or God, depending upon its use and context. The following two Radicals— (1 and 113), will demonstrate examples of this.

Another interesting feature to note is that the bronzeware radical for *complete* ♦ 14 (十) , is identical to Radical 3, *a flame of fire* ◊ (丶). This would seem to further confirm that the "complete" person was also "perfect," or holy.

In the Bible, the number ten indicates God's completeness and perfection. This implies that nothing is lacking. An example is God's ten commandments (Exodus 20: 2-17) which are ten perfect and complete rules for mankind.

Radical 1 (2)

Oracle bone Bronzeware Traditional Simplified

Definition: One; Unity, Source of all beings, first

The Beginning of Chinese Characters

Analysis: ╲ +   ╱ +   │ +   — = 푯

              Perfect   *perfect*   *perfect*   *one*   *Great Unity*

              (Person) *(Person)* *(Person)*   *(Godhead)*

Appropriately, *One, Unity, Source of all beings* —, 푯 (—) is the first discussed character in many oracle bone and bronzeware dictionaries. In the earliest oracle bone forms, we find three *perfect* (Persons) ||| 13 being united into *One* —. Notice the "Unity" expressed in the three *Ones* 푯. Furthermore, the definition: "Source of all beings" reveals Creatorship. This would appear to refer to the Trinity, or Godhead: three Divine Beings. The Hebrews had one name for God, "Elohim," which characterized plural Divine Beings. It appears that the Chinese likewise had the same concept of God—three Divine Persons acting as One. These three Persons are: God the Father; God the Son; and God the Holy Spirit. All three of these holy Persons are clearly revealed in characters, as we shall shortly see.

In the ancient Chinese writings, the Dao [the Way, Word, Truth] represents the Godhead as a whole, or any Member.¹⁵ According to Lao Zi, in the *Dao De Jing*:

The Dao exists as one. One exists as two.
Two exists as three. And three create everything.¹⁶

Again, the Creatorship is expressed. Compare the Bible:

For there are three who bear witness in heaven: the Father, the Word [Jesus Christ], and the Holy Spirit; and these three are one. (1 John 5: 7).

Radical 42

                Oracle bone Bronzeware Traditional Simplified

Definition: small, little, humble

In the Beginning—God

Analysis: This radical ｜ ｜ 17, ♦♦ 18 (小) presenting with three strokes would appear to represent the three *perfect* /|\ (十) Persons of the Godhead. Note that the bronzeware graph ♦♦ is "blackened," indicating holy.

The question arises, why should the Godhead be considered "little?" Actually, a better definition would be "humble." When Jesus Christ left heaven to be incarnated as a man, this was a tremendous demonstration of humility.

> *[Christ Jesus] who, being in the form of God, did not consider it robbery to be equal with God, but <u>made Himself of no reputation, taking the form of a servant, and coming in the likeness of men</u>. And being found in appearance as a man, He <u>humbled Himself</u> and became obedient to the point of death, even the death of the cross. (Philippians 2: 6-8).*

Furthermore, if we examine several of the oracle bone characters formed with this radical, ᄎ , ᄋ , ⼕⼕ , 19 we find members of the Godhead: the *Father* ᄋ (父 , R. 88, p. 32); the *Son* ᄋ (子 , R. 39, p. 71); and the Holy Spirit, (*Rain*) ⼕⼕ (雨 , R. 173, p. 35). Unfortunately, the meanings of these three characters are presently unknown.

Radical 113 (87, 132)   丁   丅   示   示

Oracle bone   Bronzeware   Traditional   Simplified

Definition: to manifest, demonstrate, make known, teach

Analysis: ｜   +   ⁼   =   丅
    perfect   *above*   *to manifest*
    (Person)

This radical we have come to call the "God radical" because it is the primary graph in many characters related to Divinity with significant mean-

27

The Beginning of Chinese Characters

ings, such as : blessing, auspicious, pray for, sacrifice, etc.

The most primitive oracle bone forms of this radical meaning *to manifest, demonstrate, teach* T T 20 (示) show a *perfect* | (十)Person coming from *above (heaven)* = (上). Again, this Person who came from heaven is Jesus Christ, the Son of God [see (R. 90), p. 22]. Seven hundred years before the event, it had been prophesied:

"*Behold, the virgin shall conceive and bear a Son, and shall call His name Immanuel [God with us].*" (Isaiah 7:14).

In the course of time, a young Judean maiden, Mary, engaged to be married to Joseph, a carpenter, was visited by an angel who said: "*The Holy Spirit will come upon you, and the power of the Highest will overshadow you; therefore, also, that Holy One who is to be born will be called the Son of God.*" (Luke 1: 35). Thus Jesus came, as recorded in 1 John 3: 5: "*He [Jesus] was <u>manifested</u> to take away our sins, and in Him there is no sin.*"

Jesus represented not only Himself, but also all three *perfect* /|\ Persons of the Godhead, as seen in the second form of this radical, 示 . Thus He came to earth to demonstrate the love of the Godhead for mankind. "*For in Him dwells all the fullness of the Godhead bodily.*" (Colossians 2: 19).

Radical (144)

Oracle bone Bronzeware Traditional Simplified

Definition: to bring into existence, produce, order

In the Beginning—God

Analysis: 示 + 申 = 神

"God radical"　　produce　　Shen, God,
to manifest　　　　　　　　divine

If 申 21 (申), *to produce*, is added to the "God radical" 示, we have yet a third name for the God of China—*Shen* 神 (神). The oracle bone writing 𝕊 22 (申), showing two conjoined *persons* ⺈ + ⼎ will be better understood in the following Section II, "The Beginning of the Creation of Mankind." These persons represent the first man and woman.

In the Seal (*Shuo Wen*) radical # 536 𢆉 (申), we discover the actual creation of the first *perfect* | (十) person by God's *hands* 𠂇𠂇 (爪). According to the *Shuo Wen*,

> "God (Shen) is the One who brings everything
> into existence."[23]

Therefore, *Shen* 神 is a pictogram representing the Creator-God, thus joining the other Chinese "God characters": *Shangdi* 帝 (上帝, see under R. 30, p. 21), and *Tian* 大 𠂉 (天 , see R.(90), p. 22.

Radical 160 (186)

辛　　　辛　　辛

Oracle bone　Bronzeware　Traditional　Simplified

Definition: bitter, grievous, hardship

Analysis: 丫 + 一 = 辛

Noble Man　　above　　bitter, grievous
(upside down)　(heaven)

In R 113 丅 (示) we discovered a *perfect* | Person coming down from *above* ⼆ in order to *manifest, demonstrate* ⊤ (示) what the God of heaven was really like.

> In this the love of God was <u>manifested</u> toward us, that God has sent His only begotten Son into the world, that we might live through Him. (1 John 4: 9).

In *bitter, grievous* ⾟ 24 (辛), we have another example of Jesus coming down from *above* ⼆ (上) to become a *noble* ⼤ (大) Man. Note that the *noble* ⼤ Person is coming downward as ⼭ .

But why was His life bitter and toilsome? Because of His unparalleled, virgin birth, He was ridiculed throughout life as a bastard—in spite of the ancient promise that the Savior of the world would come in this manner. A further prophecy tells of the stressful life and hardship which the Son of God must expect on earth, from the very ones He came to save:

> He is despised and rejected by
>   men,
> A Man of sorrows
>   and acquainted with grief.
>   (Isaiah 53: 3).

Although Jesus traveled about doing good, the religious leaders of Israel (Pharisees) made Him their enemy because they were jealous of the crowds that followed Him. Although confronted by bitter disappointment, He lived a humble, yet glorious life.

Radical 149 (185)

Oracle bone Bronzeware Traditional Simplified

Definition: word, speech
Analysis: ⼉ + ⼆ + ⊐ = 𠃋
    Noble Man   above   mouth   Word, speech
    (upside down)

In the oracle bone form of the previous R. 160, we found a *Noble* 人 Man descending from *above*, ⼆. We have identified Him as the Son of God, Jesus Christ, who came down from heaven to become a human, in spite of knowing that He would experience a *grievous, bitter* ⼉ (辛) life on earth. In *Word* 𠃋 25 (言), we again see the Noble Man featured with the addition of *a mouth* ⊐ , indicating creatorship. John, one of His twelve earthly disciples presented Jesus, using His name, "the Word," and wrote concerning Him:

> *In the beginning was <u>the Word</u>, and the Word was with God, and the Word was God... <u>All things were made through Him, and without Him nothing was made that was made</u>....He was in the world, and the world was made through Him, and the world did not know Him. He came to His own, and His own did not receive Him... And the <u>Word became flesh and dwelt among us</u>, and we beheld His glory, the glory as of the only begotten of the Father, full of grace and truth. (John 1: 1, 3, 10, 11, 14)*

The ancient sage, Lao Zi (老子 c.570 B.C.), described Jesus as the Dao [Way, <u>Word</u>] without realizing it:

> **Perhaps <u>He is the source of myriads of things</u>**
> **I do not know His name**
> **Call Him Dao [the <u>Word</u>]**
> **For lack of a better word, I call him**
> **"The Almighty."**[26]

Radical 135 (177)

凷 凷 舌 舌

Oracle bone　Bronzeware　Traditional　Simplified

Definition: the tongue

Analysis: 丫 + ㄩ = 凷

　　　　　Great Unity　mouth　tongue

This radical is related to 丫 (一, R. 1, p. 25), as can be seen from the oracle bone symbols 凷, 凷, 凷 27 (舌). We can identify the *Great Unity* 丫 indicating the Godhead. If 凷 is inverted, we discover *God, Tian* 穴 (天), R. (90, p. 22). In the *tongue* 凷 , the Great Unity is further specified by three small strokes ∴ , suggesting again, the Godhead. In the bronzeware graph 凷 , the three dots are replaced by ∴ (水), indicating water, the "water of life." (See R. 85, p. 192).

The Tongue, like the *mouth* ㄩ (R. 30, p. 21) and the preceding radical, *Word* 凷 (R. 149), also has reference to God's creative work.

> *When He spoke, and it was done;*
> *He commanded, and it stood fast.*
> *(Psalm 33: 9).*

Radical 88 (108)

⺈ 𠂆 父 父

Oracle bone　Bronzeware　Traditional　Simplified

Definition: Father

Analysis: ⺈ (oracle bone); 𠂆 (bronzeware)

To whom do the graphs for *Father* ⺈ 28 , 𠂆 29 ( ) refer? These graphs, frequently featured in the ancient Chinese characters, may refer to either God the Father, or to Jesus Christ who is the ultimate Progenitor of mankind, the Creator identified in Colossians 1: 15, 16:

> He [Jesus Christ] is the image of the invisible God,...For by Him all things were created that are in heaven and that are on earth,... All things were created through Him and for Him.

A prophecy in Isaiah 9: 6.7 gives a bit of Christ's past, present and future role:

> For unto us a Child is born,
> Unto us a Son is given;
> And the government will be
>   upon His shoulder.
> And His name will be called
> Wonderful, Counselor, Mighty God,
> <u>Everlasting Father,</u> Prince of Peace.
> Of the increase of His
>   government and peace
> There will be no end. . . .

While on earth, Jesus explained, *"He who has seen Me has seen the Father." (John 14: 9).* As we begin to understand the *Great Unity* ¥ (R. 1, p. 25), the Godhead, we will see how each Member's purposes and plans are the same.

Radical 101

Oracle bone   Bronzeware   Traditional   Simplified

Definition: to use, empty, a purpose, objective

Analysis: 凷 + 𠂇 = 崗

purpose   Father   garden

The most important use of this very minor radical 凷 30 (用) is in combination with Father 𢀖. The character thus formed is beginning, Father, garden 田 31, 田 32 (甫). This symbol comprises a fortuitous combination of meanings! In the beginning, the Father [God] presented to the first human couple a beautiful garden 田 33 (田, R. 102), called Eden). Arising from the center of the *garden* 田, 田 is the Father 𢀖, Y. Note that Y is a "short-hand" form of Father in which only the upraised arms are seen, and is used in the oracle bone writing of the garden 田 radical. We will subsequently meet this symbol Y in many characters. Remember that it indicates God. Lao Zi in the Dao De Jing wrote:

> **From now back till the <u>beginning</u>**
> **His name has never changed.**
>
> **In order for the <u>Father</u> (甫) of everything**
>   **to be seen,**
> **How do I know?**
> **The likeness of the Father of everything,**
> **It is from Him [Dao].**34

> *And His name will be called*
> *Wonderful, Counselor, Mighty God,*
> *<u>Everlasting Father</u>, Prince of Peace*
>   *(Isaiah 9: 6).*

Radical 29

Oracle bone   Bronzeware   Traditional   Simplified

Definition: and, again, also, in addition to, to pardon

Analysis: This radical, *and, again, also, in addition to* in the oracle bone writing is 又 35 (又) while in the bronzeware is 又 36 (又). This graph illustrates a Person with upraised arms, and can be compared with

In the Beginning—God

Father 𝕃 (父, R. 88, p.32). From the bronzeware it is apparent that a holy Person is represented from the "blackening" of 𝕃. *And, also, in addition to* 𝟙 (又) is quite appropriate for defining another Member of the Godhead. In a *friend, companion, associate* 𝟙𝟙 37 (友), we find two Members of the Godhead together. In the graph *return, turn back* 𝕃 38 (反) we find God 𝕃 *returning* to the Holy *Mountain* 厂 (厂, R. 27, p. 108).

As previously mentioned, we will frequently encounter a third form of *Father* 𝕃 as Y in many characters, for example: *create* 丫 (生, R. 100, p. 58); *Father, garden* 田 (甫, see under R. 101, previous radical); *sheep* 丫 (羊, R. 123, p. 174), and *bullock* 丫 (牛, R. 93, p. 169). *United* 丫 39 (厽) pictures the Godhead of Three acting as One in thought and purpose.

Radical 173 (204)

⻗   雨 雨

Oracle bone Bronzeware Traditional Simplified

Definition: rain
Analysis: ─ + ||| + ⁄⁄⁄ = ⻗
           above 3 *perfect (Persons)* water rain

There are many Biblical symbols for the Holy Spirit, the third Member of the Godhead. One of these is rain ⻗ 40 (雨).

> And rejoice in the LORD your God;
> For He has given you the former <u>rain</u> faithfully,
> And He will cause the <u>rain</u> to come down for you—
> The former rain, and the latter <u>rain</u> in the first month. . . .
> And it shall come to pass afterward
> That I will pour out My <u>Spirit</u> on all flesh;. . . (Joel 2: 23, 28)

A character meaning *raindrops* ☷, ☷ 41 (霝) also refers to the Holy Spirit. The three *Persons* ☷, ◁◁◁ (口, R. 30) descending from heaven are apparent. Actually, the Holy Spirit acts as the Representative on earth today of both God the Father and God the Son. Said Jesus:

> "But the Helper, the Holy Spirit, whom the Father will send in My name, He will teach you all things, and bring to your remembrance all things that I said to you." (John 14: 26).

Radical 84 (109)

☰   气   气

Oracle bone   Bronzeware   Traditional   Simplified

Definition: breath

Analysis: In the oracle bone writing, the *breath* ☰ 42 (气, "Qi") was simply designated by three horizontal strokes —very likely representing the three Persons ||| of the Godhead, just as the numeral *three* ☰ does. But the *breath* ☰ must especially represent the Holy Spirit, the third Member of the Godhead. Righteous Job of ancient times said,

> "All the while my breath is in me, and the spirit of God is in my nostrils."
> (Job 27: 3, KJV).

Here God's Spirit is equated with His life-giving breath. The Hebrew word for Spirit (ruach) is often also used for breath. There will be other radicals portraying the relationship. But notice also this simple statement from an ancient Chinese writing, the *Li Ji* (禮記):

> The "Qi" (氣) is the filling of God.[43]

In the Beginning—God

John the Baptist, "cousin" of Jesus was said to *"be filled with the Holy Spirit, even from his mother's womb." (Luke 1: 15).*

Radical 59 (63)

    Shuo Wen **Traditional** **Simplified**

Definition: ("presence of God").

Analysis:

  Mathews' Chinese-English Dictionary defines this radical as "feathers, streaky," while other dictionaries fail to attempt a definition. Actually it seems that the true meaning has been lost in the contemporary Chinese, but can be easily retrieved from ancient characters containing the radical. Neither the oracle bone nor bronzeware writings have a free-standing radical, but it is found in the *Shuo Wen* Dictionary as Radical # 331, and is rather frequently found in other characters, or even in other radicals. The number *three* ≡ we feel, written ∕∕∕ represents the Godhead, the three Divine Beings, or the "presence of God."

  In R. 113, *to manifest* 示 (示) , the "presence of God" ∕∕∕ is arranged around the simple "God radical " 丁 as ⼂⼁ .

  From the ancient *Yi Jing* (易經) we read:

> **In ancient times when the sage wrote the "Yi,"**
> **he was helped by the Spirit in a mystical way**
> **to use the number three to indicate Tian [Heaven]**[44]

  As we proceed and find many examples of ∕∕∕ , it will become increasingly obvious that this symbol does, indeed, mean "the presence of God."

Radical 182 (121)

Oracle bone Bronzeware Traditional Simplified

Definition: wind, breath

Analysis: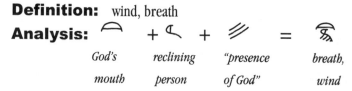

God's mouth + reclining person + "presence of God" = breath, wind

The object here is not only to show that "wind" and "breath" are synonymous, but to demonstrate that this symbol also represents the life-giving Holy Spirit. The *"Breath"* 凵 🗝 45 (風) will become more meaningful in the next section with the creation of the first human when God *"breathed into his nostrils the breath of life; and man became a living being."* (Genesis 2: 7). The 凵 graph will become clear in Section II, R. 39, with creation of the son, Adam.

Note this quotation from ancient Chinese writings that will convince us that the *Wind, Breath* is the Holy Spirit.

> "Wind (風) is the messenger of heaven and earth."
> "The Wind is to activate everything."
> "The huge breath (氣 , R. 84) is called Wind (風)."[46]

Finally, examine Jesus' words from the Bible, John 3: 8:

> "The <u>wind</u> blows where it wishes, and you hear the sound of it, but cannot tell where it comes from and where it goes. So is everyone who is born of the <u>Spirit</u>."

In the Beginning—God

In the seal characters for *wind* 🗟, 🗟 47 (風), God becomes a bending person 𠆢 ("head" drawn). The *breath* is ᘓ or ⌒ , and ☉ (日) represents the glorious first man. (See R. 72, p. 74, next Section).

Radical 172 (207)

𣥠　　　　佳　　佳

Oracle bone　Bronzeware　Traditional　Simplified

Definition: short-tailed birds, blowing of the wind, ("Holy Spirit")

Analysis:　　𝒟　+　 ⑴⑴　=　𣥠

　　　　　　mouth　"*presence of God*"　*bird, "Spirit"*

It is obvious that this new radical, *bird, wind* 𣥠 48 (佳) is very similar to the previous R. 182, *wind, breath* 🗟 (風). Again it seems that the activating breath is found. But how can a bird represent the Holy Spirit? Let us view the scene of Jesus Christ's baptism by John the Baptist in the Jordan River.

> *And John bore witness, saying, "I saw <u>the Spirit descending from heaven like a dove</u>, and He remained upon Him. I did not know Him, but He who sent me to baptize with water said to me, 'Upon whom you see the Spirit descending, and remaining on Him, this is He who baptizes with the Holy Spirit.' And I have seen and testified that this is the Son of God."*
> *(John 1: 32-34).*

So it was that the Holy Spirit worked closely with Jesus throughout His human life and ministry. Likewise, Jesus would have each of His followers be filled with the the same Holy Spirit.

The Beginning of Chinese Characters

Radical 4 (4)

Shuo Wen **Traditional** **Simplified**

Definition: a dash; downstroke to the left; (breath?)

Analysis: There are neither oracle bone nor bronzeware forms. The *Shuo Wen* # 447 symbol looks like the "breath" as found in *to speak* 49 (曰), showing the breath coming from the *speaking* (曰 R. 73) mouth. Note also this figure in the seal character, *breath* (風. see the previous radical, R. 182). (There are a total of 14 *Shuo Wen* graphs for this one radical)!

Again the breath is seen in the seal form of *to produce, life* 50 (生, R. 100, p 58). The breath is essential for life, see R. 84, p. 36.

Testified the ancient man of the east, Job, of whom the Bible says that he was "*blameless and upright*" *(Job 1:1)*:

"The <u>Spirit of God</u> has made me,
And the <u>breath of the Almighty gives me life.</u>"
(Job 33: 4)

Radical 73 (104)

Oracle bone **Bronzeware** **Traditional** **Simplified**

Definition: to speak

Analysis: to speak  51, 52 (曰), of course shows a mouth (口) but in addition, also depicts the breath arising from the mouth. In the bronzeware figure , the breath as well as the

In the Beginning—God

blackened three dots ⩙ suggest the Godhead. Therefore the speaking 㗊 represents the words of the Godhead.

Note especially one seal graph ⊖ 53 (曰) with the breath ⌒ arising from the mouth ⊔ .

Radical 183

非 非 飛

Seal writing Traditional Simplified

Definition: to fly, go quickly, high and lofty

Analysis: All the definitions of this unusual radical accurately define the Trinity—especially the Holy Spirit:, *to fly, go quickly, high and lofty*. We could find no oracle bone or bronzeware equivalent for it, however. But there are interesting seal writings: 非 非 54 (飛), which will need to be explained. In 非, we find the simplest form of the "God radical" 丅 (示), surrounded by God's *hands* 彐 (爪, R. 87, p. 24). These *hands* 彐 look almost like wings, or they could represent the *"presence of God"* ∕∕ (R. 59, p. 37), according to our interpretation.

In the rendition 非, the "God radical" 丅 is replaced by 勹 , representing a bowing *Person* . If a "head" is drawn on the figure as 勹, the Person is seen more clearly. So actually, the ancient Chinese portrayed the Godhead, represented by the *hands* 彐 working (creating) as one Person. An additional seal depiction 㣲 reveals God's *hands* 彐 and "breath" ⅋ , His means of creation .

41

The Beginning of Chinese Characters

Radical 111 (148)

Oracle bone Bronzeware Traditional Simplified

Definition: arrow, dart, aim at, pledge

Analysis: Here is yet another symbol that must surely represent the Holy Spirit! How can we be certain that the *arrow* , 55 , 56 (矢) represents the Spirit?

The oracle bone and the bronzeware radical tell us that we are dealing with a member of the Godhead because of the ◊ (see R. 3, p. 23) in the first figure, and the "blackening" of the other (see , R. (90), p. 22). Note especially how the "head" is cleverly divided into three flames in the graph . In the Bible, this verse gives a clue to this pictographic symbol:

> He [LORD] made My mouth like a sharpened <u>sword</u>,
>   In the shadow of his hand he hid me;
> He made me into a polished <u>arrow</u>
>   And concealed me in his quiver. (Isaiah 49: 2 [NIV]).

The "arrow" and "sword" are parallel in this verse. Now examine Ephesians 6: 17:

> And take the helmet of salvation, and the
> <u>sword of the Spirit</u>, which is the word of God.

Let us examine the next two related radicals to see if this interpretation is borne out.

In the Beginning—God

Radical 133 (171)

      Oracle bone Bronzeware Traditional Simplified

Definition: to reach, arrive at, greatest, best

Analysis: In 五十七 and 五十八 (至) we find the Spirit *Arrow* (矢 , R. 111) *arriving* (至) at the earth —, while 五十九 portrays Him *reaching* heaven —.

This radical again reveals attributes of the Holy Spirit—His "coming and going," as well as His superlative attributes. Specific descents of the Holy Spirit are recorded in the Bible:

> Then Jesus, when He had been baptized, came up immediately from the water; and behold, the heavens were opened to Him, and He saw <u>the Spirit of God descending</u> like a dove and alighting upon Him. And suddenly a voice came from heaven, saying, "This is My beloved Son, in whom I am well pleased."
>
> (Matthew 3: 16, 17).

When Jesus was on earth, He promised His disciples,

> "The Helper, <u>the Holy Spirit, whom the Father will send</u> in My name, He will teach you all things, and bring to your remembrance all things that I said to you."
>
> (John 14: 26).

The gift of the Holy Spirit to His followers was Christ's *greatest, best* (至) gift, for the Spirit empowered them in their understanding of the sacred Scriptures. Said Jesus:

> "When He, the Spirit of truth, has come,
> He will guide you into all truth...and
> He will tell you things to come [prophecy]."
>
> (John 16: 13).

The Beginning of Chinese Characters

Radical 56 (55)

 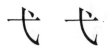

　　　　　Oracle bone Bronzeware Traditional Simplified

Definition: a dart, shoot with bow and arrow

Analysis: The *arrow* ↑ (矢 R. 111) and the *dart* 夨 60 (弋) may be used interchangeably, not only in the Chinese, but also in the Hebrew (*chets*), and Greek *(belos)*.

　　The oracle bone calligraphy is especially specific. In 夨 we recognize the three *Persons* 吕 (口 , R.30) of the Godhead. As pointed out in the discussion of *arrow* ↑ (矢 , R. 111, p. 42), this symbol indicates the Holy Spirit who is the divine Agent for God the Father, and God the Son. In the Old Testament of the Bible, the third member of the Godhead is referred to as "the Spirit of God" (e.g. Genesis 1: 1; 1 Samuel 10: 10), or the "Spirit of the Lord" (e.g. Judges 11: 12; Isaiah 11: 2), showing His "agency" or representation.

Radical 67 (84)

　　　　　Oracle bone Bronzeware Traditional Simplified

Definition: elegant, intelligent, literature, (Holy Spirit)

Analysis: This radical has been rather a puzzle. It obviously represents a person—but whom? At first, we thought it was Adam, the first "intelligent, refined" person—in contrast to evolutionary thinking that the first human was ape-like.

　　So, let us examine the oracle bone renditions of *elegant, refined* 夨 , 夨, 夨 61 (文) . Contrast the 夨 form with 至 (至 , R. 133), both

44

showing descending figures. *Arrow* ↑ (R. 111), we have analyzed as the Holy Spirit, with good reason. Another character, *to communicate, deliver* ↑ 62 (交) is also surprisingly symbolized by the arrow ↑ in the oracle bone writing. "Communication" is surely the work of the Holy Spirit.

Then, examine closely 𝄞 and note that the "chest" is divided into ◇ + ◇ + ◇ (R. 3) *flame* symbols, representing the Godhead.

That 𝄞 (文) is a member of the Godhead is confirmed in a second radical *all alike* ✦✦ (齊 Radical 210, p. 107). In the bronzeware graph 𝄞 63 (文), we find that the Holy Spirit has a special *heart* ♡ (心 R. 61, p. 109) for the first human couple.

Radical 25 (16)

卜   卜   卜

Oracle bone   Bronzeware   Traditional   Simplified

Definition: to divine, foretell, [God] chooses, ("God")

Analysis: We frequently observe this symbol, *to divine, foretell, "God"* 卜 64 (卜) representing God, as may be suggested from its use. For example: *to divine, prophesy* 占 65 (占) shows 卜 speaking with the *mouth* ▽ (口).

We can compare its use in the bronzeware character, *vessel* ⟨·⟩ 66 ⟨·⟩ 67 (卣), that refers to the enclosed man of *clay* ⟘ (土 , R. 32, p. 68), the perfect ♦ (十 , R. 24, p. 25) man, that the God-figure appears to be creating. (See the next Section on the Creation).

Radical 5 (7)

Definition: one, the second, bent, curved (breath? Holy Spirit?)

Analysis: The oracle bone ∫ 68 and bronzeware ∫ 69 (乙) graphs are identical with other graphs already shown for "breath" ⌒ as in R. 182 (風); R. 4 ⌒ (丿); as also seen in R. 73 (日).

The Holy Spirit often acts as a second Person of the Godhead. The blackening of the bronzeware graph ∫ for second surely suggests holiness, as mentioned previously.

Radical 65

Definition: a branch, descendants

Analysis: Although we've been unable to trace an oracle bone graph for branch, it does have a bronzeware form 攴 70 (支). Interestingly, the radical, second ∫ (乙 , R. 5) is attached to the radical for Father 攴 (父 , R. 88, p. 32). Does this mean that the Holy Spirit is working with the Father (Jesus Christ, in this instance. See discussion of "Father" under R. 88)? We read that Jesus was "filled" with the Holy Spirit:

> Then *Jesus, being filled with the Holy Spirit,* returned from the Jordan and was led by the Spirit... (Luke 4: 1).

We also learn that one of symbols for Jesus in the Old Testament of the Bible was "the Branch":

In the Beginning—God

> "Behold, the days are coming,"
> says the LORD,
> "That I will raise to David
> a <u>Branch</u> of righteousness; . . .
> Now this is His name by
> which He will be called:
> THE LORD
> OUR RIGHTEOUSNESS."
> (Jeremiah. 23: 5, 6).

The next two radicals (66 and 79) also depict this interesting "appendage."

Radical 66 (65,113)

Oracle bone   Bronzeware   Traditional   Simplified

Definition: to rap, tap (Father-God + Holy Spirit ?)

Analysis: The currently-used definition of this radical must have come from the appearance of the radical that seems to be a hand holding a knobbed stick for a "knocker" with which to rap or tap. However, as we study the earlier oracle bone forms ⟨ , ⟨ , ⟨ 71 (攴) and the bronzeware ⟨ 72 (攴), there appears to be the possibility that there is an "appendage" ⟨ , ⟨ , ⟨ on the radical, *Father* ⟨ , ⟨ (父, R. 88, p. 32; R. 29, p. 34). Could this "Helper" be the Holy Spirit? For example: ⟨ , corresponds to ⟨ (矢 , R. 111, p. 42).

Examine the character *similar to, like* ⟨ 73 (效) in the oracle bone and ⟨ 74 in the bronzeware. This radical ⟨ (又 , R. 29, p. 34) by itself in the oracle bone may mean *Father* ⟨ (父), while ⟨ in both indicates *arrow*.

47

In *reason, cause* (攸), the *Father* again has the "Helper" (the Holy Spirit?) . The *Person* (人 , R. 9) could represent Jesus Christ in human form. In *to work at, apply oneself* (攻), the additional *Person* is again identified.

This is not the only radical showing this phenomenon. We will next examine Radical 79 (see also R. 65, p. 46).

Radical 79 (119)

 殳 殳

Oracle bone Bronzeware Traditional Simplified

Definition: a kind of weapon, to kill

Analysis: Again in the oracle bone and bronzeware characters, we have multiple examples of the *Father*-God in combination with an appendage , , [74] (殳) which pictographically appears to be a *Person* , , ; or *God* (甫 , see R. 101); an *arrow* (矢 , R. 111, p. 42); or the breath (see under R. 182, p. 38),—all attached to (又 , R. 29, p. 34). These are all are transcribed as 殳 . It seems quite apparent that the meaning of this radical relates to the Godhead, rather than killing!

In one character alone, *sort, kind, class* , , , (般), the various forms can be seen. Why should the Father-God have these figures intimately attached, if there were not another *Person* of the Godhead working with Him in the creation of a *vessel* (舟, R. 137)? See full discussion under R. 137, Section II, p. 90, where the "*vessel*" appears to be the first couple, rather than a boat. Note how clearly the *Shuo Wen* Radical 86 portrays the second Person (kneeling).

In the Beginning—God

Radical 19 (28)

Oracle bone   Bronzeware   Traditional   Simplified

Definition: Strength, power, force

Analysis: Is not ✓ 75 (力), as seen in both the oracle bone and bronzeware figures, an arm and hand? When referring to God's strength and power in the Bible, the symbol of His arm is often used.

> *Thus says the Lord of hosts, the God of Israel... "I have made the earth, the man and the beast that are on the ground, by My great <u>power</u> and by <u>My outstretched arm</u>, and have given it to whom it seemed proper to Me.   (Jeremiah 27: 5).*

God's strong right arm ✓ (力) is also often referred to:
> You [God] have a mighty arm;
> Strong is Your hand,
>   and high is Your right hand.
>   (Psalm 89: 13)

God is personified by His strength, as in *united forces* 𝍠 76 (劦). Here we find three right arms of *Power* 𝍠 , again indicating the Godhead who were united as One in creating our earth and all life in it.

Radical 21 (39)

    ヒ   ヒ

Oracle bone   Bronzeware   Traditional   Simplified

Definition: spoon (a person)

Analysis: Although today this radical 77 (ヒ) may mean a spoon

49

or ladle, it is obvious from the ancient forms that this symbol originally represented *a person,* either God, or man, made in God's image.

For example: the character *imperial decree* 🙶 78 (旨) must have originally referred to God, the *Person* 🙶 (人 , R. 9) who *spoke* 🙶 (曰 , R. 73, p. 40) things into existence during creation of all things on the earth, and gave the first imperial decrees.

On the other hand, *to separate, turn the back side* 🙶 79 (北) must have referred to the first human man and woman (Compare with R. 81, p. 80).

The same could be said for *to change, influence, transform* 🙶 80 (化). This character reminds us of 🙶 (申), picturing the first man and woman and used in forming the character *Shen, God* 🙶 (神 , see R. (144), p. 28).

That the ancient Chinese invented more than thirty radicals related to their original concepts of God is astounding! This can only indicate their profound reverence, awe and love for their Creator-God as they attempted to preserve a knowledge and appreciation of Him for later generations. Through daily use of their written language, there was a constant reminder of the God of Heaven. And how successful these venerable Chinese scribes were by incorporating sacred knowledge for everyday use into their character-writing, for this ancient hieroglyphic writing has been used for over 4,000 years!

Sadly, however, their dedicated effort in safeguarding their original religious heritage and understanding, incorporated into their writing, was thwarted and lost for more than two millennia, as has been an appreciation of their original God. But now, their purpose can once more be realized and the true meanings of the radicals retrieved and appreciated.

1 Chung-kuo k'e-hsueh-yuan k'ao-ku yen-chiu-so, Chia-Ku Wen-Pien (Peking: K'ao-ku-hsueh chuan-k'an yi- chung ti-shih-ssu hao, 1965), p. 1.2. [Hereafter abbreviated CKWP].
2 Ibid., no. 1.2.
3 James Legge, The Notions of the Chinese Concerning God and Spirits (Hong Kong: 1852), no. 29. {Hereafter abbreviated Notions].
4 CKWP, no. 1.1.
5 Hung Pei Chiang, *Ching Wen P'ien Ching Wen* (Taipei: Kung I Publ. Co., 1974) no. 1.2 [Hereafteabbreviatead HPC].
6 Kang Xi Dictionary (Taipei: Da Shen Publ., 1978), p. 176.
7 Ibid., p. 770.
8 Lung Ch'uan Kuei T'ai Lang, Shih Chi Hui Chu K'ao Cheng (Taipei: Han Ching Wen Hua Enterprise Co., Ltd., 1983), p. 497.
9 Ethel R, Nelson, Richard Broadberry, and Ginger Chock, God's Promise to the Chinese (Dunlap: Read Books Publisher, 1997), pp. 1-6.
10 Chin Hsiang-heng, Hsu Chia-Ku Wen Pien (Taipei: I wen yin shu kuan, 1959), no. 13.8, [hereafter abbreviated HCKWP].
11 CKWP, no. 12.10; HCKWP, no. 12.12.
12 CKWP, no 9.4; HCKWP, no. 9.4.
13 CKWP, no. 3.2; HCKWP, no. 3.3.
14 Hung Pei Chiang, Ching Wen P'ien Ching Wen (Taipei: Kung I Publ. Co., 1974), no. 3.2. [Hereafter abbreviataed HPC].
15 Samuel Wang and Ethel R. Nelson, God and the Ancient Chinese (Dunlap, TN: Read Books Publ., 1999) "Unlocking the Mystery of the Dao," pp. 61-71.
16 Gia Fu Feng and Jane English, Translation of Lao Zi: Tao Te Ching (Toronto: Vintage Books, Random House, Inc. 1989), Ch. 42, p. 44.
17 CKWP, NO. 2.1.
18 HPC, NO. 2.1.
19 CKWP, no. 2.1.
20 CKWP, no. 1.3; HCKWP, no. 1.3.
21 HPC, no. 14.36.
22 CKWP, no. 14.21.
23 Kang Xi Dictionary (Taipei: Da Shen Publ., 1978), p. 770. [Hereafter abbreviated Kang Xi].
24 CKWP. No. 14.14.
25 CKWP, no, 3.4.
26 Op. Cit., Gia Fu Feng and Jane English, Ch. 25, p. 27.
27 Ma Wei Ching, Wei Ching Chia Ku Wen Yuan (Yunlin: Ma Fu Distributor, 1971), p. 729. [Hereafter abbreviataed MWC].
28 CKWP, no. 3,13.

29 HPC, no. 3.21.
30 CKWP, no. 3.31.
31 HPC, no. 3.40.
32 HCKWP, no. 3,36.
33 Ibid., no. 13.11.
34 *A Collection of 22 Classic Writers* (Shanghai: Classics Publication, 1996), p. 3.
35 CKWP, no. 3.12,
36 HPC, no. 3.20.
37 CKWP, no. 3.17.
38 HPC, no. 3.24.
39 Ibid., no. 6.10.
40 CKWP, no. 11.11.
41 Ibid. no. 11.12.
42 Op. Cit. MWP, p. 1308.
43 Wu Shuping, Lai Changyang, The Four Books and Five Jing in Modern Chinese, Vol. III (Beijing: International Culture Publishing Co, Inc., 1996), Li Ji, p. 692.
44 Kang Xi, p. 151.
45 CKWP, no. 13.3; MWC, pp. 20. 21.
46 Kang Xi, p. 1339.
47 Lin Chih Ch'ing, Ting Cheng Liu Shu T'ung (Shanghai: Kuang-I Publ. Co., 1936), section 1, p. 6. [Hereafter abbreviated LCC].
48 Op. cit., CKWP, no. 4.8.
49 Ibid., section 9, p. 26.
50 Ibid., section 6, p. 18.
51 CKWP, no,. 5.2.
52 HPC, no. 5.10.
53 LCC, Sect. 9, p. 26.
54 Lin Chih Ch'ing, Section 11, p. 11.
55 CKWP, no. 5.19.
56 HPC, no. 5.31.
57 Op. cit., no. 12.1.
58 HPC, no. 12.2.
59 MWC, p. 870.
60 Ibid. p. 869.
61 Ibid. pp. 477, 478; CKWP, no. 9.1.
62 CKWP, no. 10.14.
63 HPC, no. 9,5.
64 CKWP, no. 3.29.
65 Ibid., no. 3.30.
66 HPC, no. 7.13.
67 HPC vol, ii, p. 1158
68 CKWP, no. 14.10.
69 HPC, no. 14.22.
70 Ibid. no. 6.3.
71 MWC, p. 598.
72 HPC. No. no. 8.23.

73 MWC, p. 598.
74 HPC, no. 3.24.
75 CKWP, no. 13.10.
76 Ibid. no. 13.12.
77 CKWP, no. 8.6.
78 Ibid. no. 5.7.
79 MWC, p. 421.
80 Ibid. p. 424.

Section II

BEGINNINGS—CREATION

[Jesus said] "From the beginning of the creation, God made them male and female."   (Mark 10: 6)

Beginnings—Creation

In the previous section, we discovered that both the ancient Chinese and Hebrew peoples believed in the same Creator-God. According to the Hebrew Scriptures, God's whole creative work of producing not only our earth, but also the whole planetary system out of nothing, took only six, literal, 24-hour days.

It should be noted that God created plant life, dependent upon the sun for photosynthesis, on Day Three of earth's first week. However, He created the energy-giving sun (as well as the moon and earth's planetary system) on the fourth day. This fact proves even more conclusively that the "days" of creation were mere 24-hour periods (instead of eons of years). Plant life would be unable to survive many days without the sun's energizing rays. God's plan of creation had meaning at every juncture!

First, we will examine eight radicals picturing God bringing forth plant life from the earth.

Genesis 1: 11-19:

> *Then God said, "Let the earth bring forth grass, the herb that yields seed, and the fruit tree that yields fruit according to its kind, whose seed is in itself, on the earth"; and it was so.*
> *And the earth brought forth grass, the herb that yields seed according to its kind, and the tree that yields fruit, whose seed is in itself according to its kind. And God saw that it was good.*
> *So the evening and the morning were the third day.*
> *Then God said, "Let there be lights in the firmament of the heavens to divide the day from the night; and let them be for signs*

and seasons, and for days and years; and let them be for lights in the firmament of the heavens to give light on the earth"; and it was so.
Then God made two great lights; the greater light to rule the day, and the lesser light to rule the night. He made the stars also. God set them in the firmament of the heavens to give light on the earth, and to rule over the day and over the night, and to divide the light from the darkness.
And God saw that it was good.
So the evening and the morning were the fourth day.

Radical 100

Oracle bone Bronzeware Traditional Simplified

Definition: to produce, create, bring forth life

Analysis: *to produce, bring forth life, create* 㞢 ¹ (生) shows God 丫 (with "head" appended, ⍷ . See Father 𝔏 , R. 88, p. 32) with upraised arms, bringing forth life from the *earth, ground* _ .

From the Hebrew Scriptures recorded on the previous page, we learned that God commanded the earth to bring forth all vegetation from the ground. God created by *speaking* 告 ² (告) things into existence with His *mouth* ⊌ (口 , R. 30).

丫 + _ = 㞢 + ⊌ = 告
"God"   ground   create   mouth   to speak

Both the Chinese and Hebrews record that God brought forth life by simply speaking to the earth.

The Chinese philosopher Mo Zi (408-382 B.C.) describes the great variety of plants which He created when he wrote:

Beginnings—Creation

Even the tip of a hair is the work of Tian [Heaven, God].
Tian [Heaven 天] sent down snow, frost, rain and dew to grow the five grains and flax and silk so that the people could use and enjoy them. ³

We find that the ancient Chinese used radical graphs for seven plants, that He created on Day Three:

Radical 45 (61)

Ψ   Υ   ΨΙ   Ψ

Oracle Bone Bronzeware Traditional Simplified

Definition: beginning of everything, plants sprouting
Oracle bone: Ψ ⁴ ; Bronzeware: Υ ⁵ ; Shuo Wen # 11: Ψ ⁶.

Radical 140

↓↓   ↓↓   ─╫─

Oracle Bone Bronzeware Traditional Simplified

Definition: grass, herbs, weeds, hasty, beginnings of things

Oracle bone: ↓↓ ⁷ ; Bronzeware: ↓↓ ⁸ ; Shuo Wen # 12: ΥΥ ⁹.

Radical 202

Oracle Bone Bronzeware Traditional Simplified

Definition: glutinous millet

Oracle bone: 㣇 [10] ; Bronzeware: 秫 [11] ; Shuo wen # 255: 黍 [12] .

Radical 119 (159)

Oracle Bone　Bronzeware　Traditional　Simplified

Definition: hulled rice, uncooked rice, grain

Oracle bone: 米 [13] ; Bronzeware: 米 [14] ; Shuo Wen # 257: 米 [15] .

Radical 199 (188)

Oracle Bone　Bronzeware　Traditional　Simplified

Definition: wheat

Oracle bone: 来 [16] ; Bronzeware: 來 [17] ; Shuo Wen # 197: 麥 [18] .

Radical 118 (178)

Oracle Bone　Bronzeware　Traditional　Simplified

Definition: bamboo

Oracle bone: 竹 [19] ; Bronzeware: ; Shuo Wen # 143: [20] .

Beginnings—Creation

Radical 200

麻麻麻

Oracle Bone Bronzeware Traditional Simplified

Definition   hemp, numb, drugged

Oracle bone: ; Bronzeware: 麻 ²¹ ; Shuo Wen # 263 麻 ²² .

Next in the Creator-God's agenda was to form animals on Day Five to inhabit the waters and air! Five of these are memorialized in radicals.

Genesis 1: 20-23:

> Then God said, "Let the waters abound with an abundance of living creatures, and let birds fly above the earth across the face of the firmament of the heavens."
> So God created great sea creatures and every living thing that moves, with which the waters abounded, according to their kind, and every winged bird according to its kind. And God saw that it was good.
> And God blessed them, saying, "Be fruitful and multiply, and fill the waters in the seas, and let birds multiply on the earth.".So the evening and the morning were the fifth day.

Radical 195 (209)

魚 魚 魚 鱼

Oracle Bone Bronzeware Traditional Simplified

Definition: a fish

Oracle bone: 魚 ²³ ; Bronzeware: ²⁴ ; Shuo Wen # 424: 魚 ²⁵ .

61

Radical 213

Oracle Bone   Bronzeware   Traditional   Simplified

Definition: a tortoise, longevity
Oracle bone: 26 ; Bronzeware: 27 ;
Shuo Wen # 476: 28 .

Radical 205

Oracle Bone   Shuo Wen   Traditional   Simplified

Definition: a toad, frog, to strive, endeavor
Oracle bone: 29 ; Bronzeware: ;
Shuo Wen # 119: 30 .

Radical 196

Oracle Bone   Bronzeware   Traditional   Simplified

Definition: a bird
Oracle bone 31 ; Bronzeware: 32 Shuo Wen # 119: 33 .

Then, on the sixth day, God first focused His attention to creating the myriads of land animals, as recorded in the Bible. Six of these are pictured in radicals.

Genesis 1: 24, 25:

God said, "Let the earth bring forth the living creature according to its kind: cattle and creeping thing and beast of the earth, each according to its kind"; and it was so.
And God made the beast of the earth according to its kind, cattle according to its kind, and everything that creeps on the earth according to its kind. And God saw that it was good.

Radical 141 (173)

Oracle Bone   Shuo Wen   Traditional   Simplified

Definition: a tiger, emblem of bravery

Oracle bone: [34] ; Bronzeware: [35] ; Shuo Wen # 167: [36] .

It would appear that the Godhead is contained within this radical, especially in the bronzeware and Shuo Wen graphs. In 虎 , we find ∧ + ∨ + ∕ = ✕ . A similar figure we will meet in worker of miracles 由 (巫), where ⊢ + T + ⊣ represent three "God radicals" T (示, R. 113). In the Shuo Wen radical 虎 , we again find three figures: ⊏ + ⊏ + ⊐ , which would seem to represent the Godhead. However, there is no biblical application of the Godhead to a tiger—to a lion, yes, but not a tiger. There has, however, been some geomancy (divination) application of the tiger.

Radical 94

    Oracle Bone Bronzeware Traditional Simplified

Definition: a dog

Oracle bone: [37]; Bronzeware: [38]; Shuo Wen # 377: [39].

Radical 198 (221)

    Oracle Bone Bronzeware Traditional Simplified

Definition: a deer, stag

Oracle bone: [40]; Bronzeware: [41];
Shuo Wen # 372: [42].

Radical 187 (75)

    Oracle Bone Bronzeware Traditional Simplified

Definition: a horse, at once, immediately, rapidly

Oracle bone: [43]; Bronzeware: [44]; Shuo Wen # 370 [45].

Radical 152 (194)

    Oracle Bone Bronzeware Traditional Simplified

Definition: a pig, hog

Oracle bone: [46]; Bronzeware: [47]; Shuo Wen # 362: [48].

Beginnings—Creation

Radical 208 (224)

  鼠 鼠

Oracle Bone   Bronzeware   Traditional   Simplified

Definition: a rat, mouse, squirrel, mole, hidden, secret

Oracle bone: 49 ; Bronzeware: ; Shuo Wen # 379: 50 .

Now it was time for God's crowning work of creation: Mankind!

Genesis 1: 26- 31:

> *Then God said, "Let Us make man in Our image, according to Our likeness; let them have dominion over the fish of the sea, over the birds of the air, and over the cattle, over all the earth and over every creeping thing that creeps on the earth."*
> *So God created man in His own image; in the image of God He created him; male and female He created them.*
> *Then God blessed them, and God said to them, "Be fruitful and multiply; fill the earth and subdue it; have dominion over the fish of the sea, over the birds of the air, and over every living thing that moves on the earth."*
> *And God said, "See, I have given you every herb that yields seed which is on the face of all the earth, and every tree whose fruit yields seed; to you it shall be for food.*
> *"Also, to every beast of the earth, to every bird of the air, and to everything that creeps on the earth, in which there is life, I have given every green herb for food"; and it was so.*
> *Then God saw everything that He had made, and indeed it was very good. So the evening and the morning were the sixth day.*

Genesis 2: 7:

> *And the LORD God formed man of the dust of the ground, and breathed into his nostrils the breath of life; and man became a living being.*

There are several things to especially notice in this Biblical record, that will actually be brought out as the Radicals are studied in detail:

- Note that "God" (Elohim) is plural: "Let Us;" "Our" image; "Our" likeness. We have just studied in Section I about the Godhead of three Persons: God the Father, God the Son, and God the Holy Spirit.
- Mankind was created "in the image of God," Himself.
- God formed man from the dust of the earth.
- Man received life only after God breathed into his nostrils the "breath of life."
- God specified man's diet.
- Man was given dominion over the entire earth and its contents.
- Everything that God made was "very good." The work of creation ended on the sixth day of that first week.

Now we will begin our study of the Chinese Radicals that are related to the creation of mankind—both male and female, and see how closely these 36 graphs follow the ancient Hebrew Biblical record.

Radical 37 (52)   大   大   大   大

Oracle Bone   Bronzeware   Traditional   Simplified

Definition: noble [man]; great, almighty

Analysis: This radical is a pictograph of a *noble, great* 大 [51] (大) person, and can represent not only the first created man, but also woman [Adam and his wife]. Note the similarity to *God, Heaven* 天 [天, R. (90)], in whose image they were created.

> *So God created man in His own image;*
> *in the image of God He created him;*
> *male and female He created them.*
>   *(Genesis 1:27).*

Beginnings—Creation

This God [Jesus Christ] later came from heaven to earth as a man, so *Noble* 大 may, on occasion, also refer to Jesus. (See also Radicals 24, 113, 160, 149, 88, etc.).

Said Lao Zi:

> **I do not know His name.**
> **Name Him "Dao" (** 道 **) possibly.**
> **For lack of a better word,**
> **I call Him "The Almighty" (** 大 **).**⁵²

Radical 9 (21, 23)

Oracle Bone Bronzeware Traditional Simplified

Definition: a man, mankind, person

Analysis: As with the radical, *noble, great* 大 (大, R. 37), so the radical *man, person* ⁵³ (人) can represent Adam, the earthly man, or Jesus, the Heavenly Man in whose image Adam was created. The character may be more clearly identified as a person in the profile graph if a "head" is appended, as .

The character, *beginning* ⁵⁴ (元), shows the heavenly *Man* [Jesus Christ] who would one day come down from heaven *above* (上).

> *The first man was of the earth, made of dust;*
> *the second Man is the Lord from heaven.*
>   *(1 Corinthians 15: 47).*

Radical 10 (29)

Oracle Bone Bronzeware Traditional Simplified

Definition: a man, person

Analysis: This radical does not have a unique graph in the oracle bone form, but has been identified as identical to *man* 𠂇 (人) in contemporary writing, e.g. (元). It becomes clear that the oracle bone form of in this character is thus 𠂇 ⁵⁵ (儿).

Radical 83 (122)

Oracle Bone Bronzeware Traditional Simplified

Definition: family, clan

Analysis: In the graph, *family, clan* ⁵⁶ (氏), the *Person* 𠂇 represents Tian [*God, Heaven*] [天 , R. (90)] who is forming a man in His own glorious, holy image, represented by a *flame* ◊ (丶 , R. 3, p. 23). Earth's first man, from whom all *families* 氏 are ultimately derived, originally had God's perfect, sinless character.

𠂇   +   ◊   =   氏

Person   flame   family, clan
(God)   "holy"

Radical 32 (49)

Oracle Bone Bronzeware Traditional Simplified

Definition: earth, soil

Analysis: ◊   +   —   =   土

"holy" flame   "ground"   earth, soil (Adam)

The radical, *earth, soil* 土 ⁵⁷ (土) shows God's holy attribute ◊ (丶 , R. 3, R. 83) being transferred to the man of *earth* 土 that He formed from the ground — .

Beginnings—Creation

> *And the LORD God formed man of the <u>dust of the ground</u>,*
> *And breathed into his nostrils the breath of life;*
> *And man became a living being. (Genesis 2: 7)*

God named the first man "Adam," meaning in Hebrew "ground," "clay," and also "red." The "breath of life" appears to have been administered by the Holy Spirit.

> *You take away their breath,*
>   *they die and return to their*
>   *dust.*
> *You send forth Your Spirit,*
>   *they are created;*
>   *(Psalm 104: 29, 30).*

See the discussion of the "breath" ∫ (under R. 4; also R. 84; R. 182).

Observe that in the character meaning great, good 𠆢 58 (壬), a man 𠆢 arises from the earth, soil ◯ . That man, Adam, was indeed great and good initially, for God's hands had imparted holiness (聖 , see R.3) to him.

Radical 33 (49)

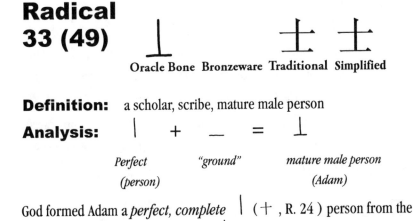

Oracle Bone   Bronzeware   Traditional   Simplified

Definition: a scholar, scribe, mature male person

Analysis: | + — = ⊥

     Perfect   "ground"   mature male person
     (person)   (Adam)

God formed Adam a *perfect, complete* | (十 , R. 24) person from the ground — , a *mature male person* ⊥ 59 (士). God completed the creative process by breathing into his nostrils "the breath of life." In the Zhou dynasty, the meaning of 丄 is a "mature male person," which confirms our initial hypothesis that ∣ (十) symbolizes a *perfect* person. (See Section I: R. 24, R. 1, R. 42, R. 113, R. 144).

Historically, there was always a class of scribes 丄 (土) who taught the Chinese classical writings, gave counsel to rulers, and were regarded as the conscience of society.

Radical 48 (48)   工   工 工
Oracle Bone Bronzeware Traditional Simplified

Definition: work, labor, workman

Analysis: 丅 + 口, 丄 = 舀, 工
God   mature male person   work, labor

The graph 工 [60] (工), meaning *work, workman* pictures God 丅 (示, R. 113) as an artisan creating the *mature male person* 丄 (土, R. 33), Adam.

Regarding *worker of magic* 坪 (巫): this character is now associated with everything evil: mysticism, magic, spiritualism—but surprisingly the original meaning presents a totally different picture. It would seem that the ancient Chinese considered God 丅 as a *Worker of miracles* 坪 [61] (巫) in His creative activity. For in 坪 we find the Godhead (Trinity) portrayed as ⊢丅⊣ (compare with 示, R. 113) where the three divine Persons are working together to form the *mature male person* 丄, Adam.

Radical 117 (126)   立 立
Oracle Bone Bronzeware Traditional Simplified

Beginnings—Creation

Definition: to stand up, establish, create, start

Analysis: 大 + — = 立

             Noble, great   *ground*   *create, stand,*
             (person)   *establish*

The radical *to create, found, establish, stand up* 立 [62] (立) pictures a *noble* 大 (大 , R. 37) person standing on the ground — . This radical has a number of significant meanings: *to establish, create, start, found, stand up*—all of which picture Adam <u>standing innocent before God</u>. Mankind was established blameless and perfect at the start.

Said Jesus: *"Watch therefore, and pray always that you may be counted worthy. . . to stand before the Son of Man."(Luke 21: 36).*

> **The Dao [way] for a man to stand
> is by love and righteousness.**[63]

Radical 39 (74)

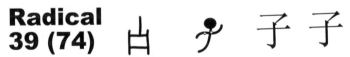

Oracle Bone   Bronzeware   Traditional   Simplified

Definition: a son, child, offspring, seed, bride, wife

Analysis: 凵 + | = 出

          Breath   *perfect*   *offspring, son*
          (of God)   *(person)*

This radical has two very different oracle bone forms: *offspring, son, child, seed* 凵 [64], 子 [65] (子), which require some explanation. You may recall that 凵 (風 , R. 182) is one symbol for *breath*, often indicating the life-giving breath of God. In *son* 出 , we find God's *breath* 凵 entering the *perfect* | (十 , R. 24) person, Adam. We should also review, at this point

The Beginning of Chinese Characters

the alternate graph for *breath, wind* 🗲 (風 , see R. 182).

$$\frown + \triangleleft + \equiv\!\!\!\equiv\ =\ 🗲$$

God's mouth   reclining person   "God's presence"   breath
                 (Adam)

After God had formed Adam of clay, the breath of God entered his reclining body, energizing his body to life. *"And the LORD God formed man of the dust of the ground, and <u>breathed into his body the breath of life,</u> and man became a living being. (Genesis 2:7).*

The second graph, 孚 for *son, offspring,* appears to have a similar original meaning. Using another character for *breath* in the oracle bone writing 丁 [66] (丂), and 口 (丁), meaning *person, adult male.*

$$丁\ +\ 口\ =\ 孚$$

    breath   person   son, offspring

After his creation, God had *trust, confidence* 孚 [67] (孚) in Adam. This shows God's *hand* ㇇ (爪 , R. 87) extended over the *son* 孚 .

The Son may also represent the Son of God, and as such was written as 子 [68] (子) with "God's presence" ≡ (彡 , R. 59), written as 彡 adorning Him. The bronzeware 子 [69] , by its "blackening" also denotes holiness.

The sixth day of earth's first week was full of animation, and many Chinese radicals reflect this activity! The Hebrew Scriptures continue to record the various events:

Genesis 2: 7-9; 15-25:

> *And the LORD God formed man of the dust of the ground, and breathed into his nostrils the breath of life; and man became a living being[soul,KJV].*
> *The LORD God planted a garden eastward in Eden, and there*

He put the man whom He had formed.
And out of the ground the LORD God made every tree grow that is pleasant to the sight and good for food. The tree of life was also in the midst of the garden, and the tree of the knowledge of good and evil....
Then the LORD God took the man and put him in the garden of Eden to tend and keep it.
And the LORD God commanded the man, saying, "Of every tree of the garden you may freely eat;
"but of the tree of the knowledge of good and evil you shall not eat, for in the day that you eat of it you shall surely die."
And the LORD God said, "It is not good that man should be alone; I will make him a helper comparable to him."
Out of the ground the LORD God formed every beast of the field and every bird of the air, and brought them to Adam to see what he would call them. And whatever Adam called each living creature, that was its name.
So Adam gave names to all cattle, to the birds of the air, and to every beast of the field. But for Adam there was not found a helper comparable to him.
And the LORD God caused a deep sleep to fall on Adam, and he slept; and He took one of his ribs, and closed up the flesh in its place.
Then the rib which the LORD God had taken from man He made into a woman, and He brought her to the man.
And Adam said:

> *"This is now bone of my bones*
> *And flesh of my flesh;*
> *She shall be called Woman,*
> *Because she was taken out of Man."*

Therefore a man shall leave his father and mother and be joined to his wife, and they shall become one flesh.
And they were both naked, the man and his wife, and were not ashamed.

Radical 72 (103)

☉ ⊙ 日 日
Oracle Bone Bronzeware Traditional Simplified

Definition: the sun, a day, daily ("holy person?")

Analysis: ○ + • = ⊙

Person   "holy"   sun, "holy person"

This radical for *sun, day* ⊙₇₀ (日), besides representing our sun in the heavens, appears to also refer to the upright first man, Adam. For Adam was made in the image of Jesus Christ, "the Sun of Righteousness" (Malachi 4:2). Refer, for example, to the seal character for *breath* ⌒₇₁ (气) where the *breath* ☰ (气 , R. 84), appears to be giving life to Adam, the *sun* ⊙.

Next, examine *dawn* 旦 ₇₂ (旦) where the *sun* ⊙ is rising upon the *person* □ (丁). Does this indicate that Adam was formed at dawn of the sixth day of creation? Surely, Adam was very busy that first day of his life, naming all the animals as God created them. When Adam observed the animal pairs, he must have wondered, "Where's my mate?"

It was at *dusk*, ₇₃ (昏) that God provided Adam's need for a mate to marry . This is pictorially expressed as follows:

⺈ + ⊙ =

Person (God)   sun (Adam)   dusk, to marry

Radical 146 (166)

⊻ 西 西
Oracle Bone Bronzeware Traditional Simplified

Beginnings—Creation

Definition: west, western

Analysis: | + ∪ = ⊎

Perfect (person)　　mouth, person　　west
(woman)　　(Adam)

This radical, west ⊎ (西), along with several other radicals, appear to be related to the creation of the first woman. These will be discussed in sequence: R. 36 *evening*) (夕); R. 74 *moon*) (月); R. 130 *flesh* D (月); and R. 188 *bone* (骨).

So, on that wonderful sixth day of creation, as the sun was setting in the *west* ⊎ [74] (西), God created another *perfect* | (十, R. 24) person, woman, taken from the body of the first *person* ∪ (口, R. 30), Adam.

| + ∪ = ⊎

Perfect (person)　　mouth, person　　west

In a second rendition of *west* ⊎ (西), we find *two* = [75] (二) *perfect* | persons joined as one *person* ∪ (口), for the Hebrew Scriptures record that after creating Adam and his wife, God performed the first marriage ceremony.

Therefore a man shall leave his father and mother and be joined to his wife, and they shall become one flesh. (Genesis 2: 24).

Adam had *wanted, needed, desired* [76] (要) a helpmeet. Here we find God's *hands* taking the *woman* (女) from the *sunlike* (Adam) ⊙ (日, see R. 72).

hands (God's) + woman + sun (Adam) = want, need, important

75

Radical 36 (64)

　　　　　D　　　　　夕　夕

　　　　Oracle Bone　Bronzeware　Traditional　Simplified

Definition: evening, dusk

Analysis: As the sun was setting in the west, and *evening, dusk* D 77 (夕) was coming on, the Hebrew Scriptures relate:

> And the LORD God caused a deep sleep to fall on Adam, and he slept; and He took one of his ribs, and closed up the flesh in its place. Then the rib which the LORD God had taken from man He made into a woman, and He brought her to the man.
> (Genesis 2: 21, 22)

　　The character *evening, dusk*. D (夕) shows a *person, mouth* ㅂ (口) turned on its side, indicating Adam asleep, reclining that *evening* D (夕). A second version of this radical is written D (夕), and is also identical to the character, moon D , D (月 , see the next R. 74).

　　The character, *many, much* 多 78 (夕夕), indicates that from these first two persons (indicated by two *mouths* ㅂ + ㅂ), *many* 多 (夕夕) other persons would be born—the whole human race!

Radical 74 (118)

　　　　　D　　　　　月　月

　　　　Oracle Bone　Bronzeware　Traditional　Simplified

Definition: moon, month

Analysis: 　The oracle bone renditions of this radical, *moon* D ,

Beginnings—Creation

) 79 (月) are identical to R. 36 *evening, dusk*) (夕), and R. 130 (118) *flesh*) (月), evidently because of the event taking place at *dusk,* when the *moon* was rising on the sixth day of creation. Again we see a *person, mouth* ∀ (口) lying on its side as) . The event was the creation of Adam's mate from his side as he slept. In a second form of *moon* ID (月), we find an additional *perfect* | (十) person, the woman being formed from the body of Adam.

| +) = ID
Perfect (person)   *person (Adam)*   *moon*
(woman)

Radical 130

D   肉 月

Oracle Bone   Bronzeware   Traditional   Simplified

Definition: flesh

Analysis: The oracle bone graph of this radical, *flesh* D 80 (肉), is identical to both R. 36 and R. 74. It portrays a *person* ∀ (口) reclining, indicating Adam asleep. From the pictograms, we recognize that *flesh* D originally did not refer to meat, but rather to a person.

The "traditional" character form 肉 looks very different from either the oracle bone or bronzeware radicals. In a seal writing of *flesh* 🔾 81 (肉), the origin of this graph may be traced.

Ω (Ω) + 𝛑 + ♀ = 🔾
person (Adam)   *hand (God's)*   *wife*   *flesh*

Without seeing the actual creation of the woman, upon awakening, when

77

The Beginning of Chinese Characters

Adam saw the lovely person standing before him, in faith he exclaimed,

> This is now bone of my bones
> And <u>flesh of my flesh</u>;
> She shall be called Woman,
> Because she was taken out of Man.
> *(Genesis 2: 23).*

Perhaps now one can understand why the "traditional" forms of *flesh* 𐅁 (月) and *moon* 𐅀 (月) are so difficult to differentiate—they were often written the same in the original writing!

Radical 11

Oracle Bone   Bronzeware   Traditional   Simplified

Definition: to enter, inside

Analysis: This radical also describes the creation of the woman when the hand of God *entered* 人 , 人 ⁸² (入) Adam's body to take out a second *perfect, complete* 丨 (十 , R. 24) person, his wife.

An important derived character, *inside, wife* 内 ⁸³ (内) indicates that Adam's *wife* came from *inside* his body.

```
   冂     +     入     =     内
enclosure      to enter      wife, inside
(Adam's body)
```

Radical 188 (213)

Oracle Bone   Bronzeware   Traditional   Simplified

Beginnings—Creation

Definition: bone, skeleton, framework
Analysis: As with the previous radical, *flesh* (肉, R. 130), the radical *bone* ⁸⁴ (骨) shows woman, a *person, mouth* (口) arising from Adams's *bone*, namely his rib.

> Then the rib which the LORD God had taken from man He made into a woman, and He brought her to the man. (Genesis 2: 22).

When Adam had awakened after this first "surgical procedure" performed by God Himself upon his body, He was delighted with his bride, and had proclaimed,

> "This is now <u>bone of my bones</u>
> And flesh of my flesh;"
>   (Genesis 2: 23).

Radical 38 (73)

Oracle Bone Bronzeware Traditional Simplified

Definition: woman
Analysis: This radical is simply a graph of a *woman* ⁸⁵ (女), and represents the first woman, Adam's wife. This will become obvious from the study of characters containing this radical.

From the Hebrew Scriptures we learned that God *prepared* ⁸⁶ (妥) Eve to be a *suitable* helper for Adam.

+	=

Hand (God's)   woman   suitable, to prepare

> The LORD God said, "It is not good for the man to be alone; I will make a helper <u>suitable</u> for him.:" (Genesis 2: 18, NIV).

Having a *woman* in the first *home* ⁸⁷ (宀) resulted in Adam's

79

heart being at *peace* 安 88 (安). Furthermore, we later read that Adam renamed woman, "Eve."

> And Adam called his wife's name Eve, <u>because she was the mother of all living</u>. (Genesis 3: 20).

From the character *mother* 母 89 (母), we see the *woman* 女 was originally created to become a mother. She became the mother of *every, all* 每 90 (每) living persons.

Then God blessed them, and God said to them,
"Be fruitful and multiply;" (Genesis 1: 28)

Radical 81 (123)

比 比

Oracle Bone Bronzeware Traditional Simplified

Definition: to compare, liken to, be near, follow, intimate

Analysis:. Before God created the woman, He said, "*I will make a helper <u>comparable</u> to him [Adam].*" (Genesis 2: 18). The character *comparable, likened to* 比 91 (比) shows a second *person* 人 (人), his wife, likened to Adam, the first *person* 人 . After the creation of the woman, God performed the first marriage ceremony:

> "Therefore a man shall leave his father and mother and be joined to his wife, and they shall become one flesh."
> (Genesis 2: 24).

The character *unite, join* 竝 92 (立立, see R. 117) also shows the first two *noble* 大 (大) persons as a couple, hand in hand, *joined* in marriage.

Beginnings—Creation

| noble (person) | noble (person) | ground | join, unite |

Confucius said:

"**Marriage is the beginning of all generations.**"⁹³

Radical 26 (32)

      Oracle Bone   Bronzeware Traditional Simplified

Definition: a command, to forbid, (kneeling man)

Analysis: A frequently seen graph in the oracle bone writing shows a kneeling man ⁹⁴ (卩) who must have originally portrayed Adam, the first man.

When God created man in His own image, He *sealed, imprinted* ⁹⁵ (印) with His *hand* (爪 , R. 87) His own character upon the man , Adam.

But most important, God gave Adam, with His own mouth (口) a specific *command, mandate* ⁹⁶ (令).

"Of every tree of the garden you may freely eat; but of the tree of the knowledge of good and evil you shall not eat, for in the day that you eat of it you shall surely die." (*Genesis 2: 16, 17*).

In a second character meaning, *command of Tian [Heaven, God], life* ⁹⁷ (命), we find God's *mouth* (口 , R. 30), pictured upside down (and taking the shape of a mountain), pronouncing the command to the kneeling man (here standing as), and the second person

81

(the woman) not to eat of the tree of the knowledge of good and evil! The woman was also informed of the command!

△ + ▷ + ⊔ = ⊖▷
God's mouth   man   person   God's command,
              (Adam)   (woman)   life

Actually, their very *lives*  depended upon obedience to this command!

Radical 52 (76)

𠔇   幺   幺

Oracle Bone   Bronzeware   Traditional   Simplified

Definition: small, tender, alone

Analysis: The oracle bone graph for *small, tender, alone* 𠔇 [98] (幺) shows two conjoined, holy persons—that would most likely represent Adam and his wife, since they are the featured human couple portrayed in the radical pictograms. The bronzeware form of *small, tender* 𠔇 [99] (幺) leaves no doubt as to their identity, as we find the "holy" • designation on the *perfect* | [100] (十 , R. 24) persons.

The first couple's origin from the Creator-God is portrayed by the *connecting link* 𠔇, 𠔇 [101] (系) that depicts not only the couple 𠔇 , but also God's *hand* 乂 , 爫 (爪).

𠔇   +   乂   =   𠔇

small (couple)   God's hand   connecting link

We have previously identified 孑 (子 , R. 39) as Adam. Many years later, Adam and Eve could speak of their *grandsons, posterity* 孫 [102] (孫).

Beginnings—Creation

Radical 155 (190)

赤 赤

Oracle Bone   Bronzeware   Traditional   Simplified

Definition: naked, red

Analysis: To be created *"in the image of God," (Genesis 2: 7)* meant the Adam was perfect and sinless, even as Shangdi [Tian, Heaven] is perfect. Shangdi's dazzling perfection of character is spoken of as His "glory," and is represented in the Chinese graphs as *tongues of fire* ◊ (` , R. 3); as *fire* ⩔ , ⩔ , ⩔ (火 , R. 86); and as the *sun* ☉ (日 , R. 72).

> O Lord my God, You are very
>   great;
> You are clothed with honor
>   and majesty,
> Who cover Yourself with light
>   as with a garment,
>   (Psalm 104: 1, 2).

Therefore, it appears that Adam was originally clothed in a glorious fiery light, even as God. The character *naked, red* ¹⁰³ (赤) depicts Adam, the *noble* 大 (大 , R. 37) man clothed with *fire* ⩔ (火 , R. 86). *"And they were both naked, the man and his wife, and were not ashamed" (Genesis 2: 25)* because they were clothed with a glorious "robe" of *fire*. The Hebrew name "Adam" aptly means both "red" and "earth!"

大 + ⩔ =

noble (person)   fire   naked, red

Radical (172)

光 光

Oracle Bone   Bronzeware   Traditional   Simplified

83

Definition: naked, bare, light

Analysis: Here is further corroboration that Adam and his wife were originally covered by a glorious light. A second radical meaning both *naked* and *light* 𝟚, 𝟚 ¹⁰⁴ (光) show unmistakably both the *kneeling man* 𝟚 (卩 . R. 26) and the *woman* 𝟚 (女 , R. 38). They are covered by *fiery* 𝟚 , 𝟚 (火) robes.

𝟚 , 𝟚 + =

Man,   woman   fire   naked, glorious light

Radical 121 (175)

    𝟚   𝟚   缶   缶

Oracle Bone Bronzeware Traditional Simplified

Definition: pottery, earthenware

Analysis: Since God formed man from clay, it is appropriate that Adam be "labeled" as *pottery, earthenware* 𝟚 ¹⁰⁵ (缶). The oracle bone version 𝟚 shows God's *mouth* ⊔ (口) breathing the breath of life into Adam—(↑ represents the upper half of 人 , the person who had been created by God from the clay).

↑ + ⊔ = 𝟚

man   mouth   pottery
(upper half) (God's)

Adam was the "pottery;" God, the "Potter."

In the bronzeware form 𝟚 ¹⁰⁶ (缶), we see both Adam and his wife, two "holy" ♦ + ♦ , *perfect* | (十) persons. She arises from Adam. ⊔ represents God's *mouth*.

Beginnings—Creation

● + ● + ⊌ = ⍜

perfect perfect mouth   pottery

The character *kiln for burning pottery, be pleased* 匋 [107] (匋), in the bronzeware, depicts God as a workman 𠆢 (人), bending over Adam, the *mature adult male* 土 [108] (土 , R. 33), *pleased* with the vessel He is making. God's *mouth* ⊌ breathes life into Adam, the man of clay.

土 + ⊌ + 𠆢 = 匋

mature adult   mouth   Person (God)   pleased,
male   (God's)   kiln for pottery

Radical 193 (218)

鬲 鬲 鬲 鬲

Oracle Bone Bronzeware Traditional Simplified

Definition: a large earthen pot

Analysis: Since the first man Adam was formed by God from the dust (clay) of the ground, what is more fitting than a pictogram of a *large earthen pot* 鬲 [109] 鬲 , 鬲 [110] (鬲) to portray him with his wife, who arises from the side of the man. We see the two back-to-back persons as 𠆢 and ⋀ . An additional bronzeware form shows God's *hands* ⼿ working as a Potter, forming the *large earthen pot*  [111] (鬲).

In a *cooking pot* 鬶 [112] (鑊), we again find the couple ⋀ , this time on the fiery Holy Mountain ⼭ (山 , 火 R. 46 and 86). The interesting figure 𡗗 , represents the *Father* 父 (父 , R. 88) and the *Breath* 八 (see discussion under 風 , R. 182, of the Holy Spirit).

85

The Beginning of Chinese Characters

Radical 98 (98)

                Shuo Wen   Traditional   Simplified

Definition: earthenware, pottery

Analysis: Once more we have a "vessel" radical—all of which must refer to the first human "vessel(s)." (See also Radicals 121, 193, 206, 108, 151, 137). This present radical has no oracle bone or bronzeware forms, however there is a *Shuo Wen* Radical 462, *earthenware, pottery* ∋ , ⓺ *113* (瓦). The figure ∋ is formed by conjoined, "artistically-drawn" kneeling *persons* as ∈ (upside down) and ⊃ . In the second graph ⓺ , we again find conjoined figures. The person ⊃ coming from the ground — (turned right side up), may well be the "vessel," Adam; while the remaining "vessel," his wife ⊃ appears to be kneeling.. These symbols are similar to the graph ⌇ (申), *to produce,* composed of the conjoined *persons* ⌇ (one again upside down). These are a unique and beautiful way of portraying the first couple!

The character drawn of the *Shuo Wen* Radical 91, (甈), depicts the Holy Mountain symbolized by ∩ with two *Persons*)(of the Godhead above, again perhaps forming the human vessels, the *"earthenware pottery,"* ⓺ Adam and the woman.

Radical 206

            Oracle Bone Bronzeware Traditional Simplified

Definition: a tripod, sacrificial vessel indicating imperial power.

Analysis: Another graph depicts the first human couple, Adam and his wife, as God's vessels. This one must have great significance: *a sacrifi-*

Beginnings—Creation

cial vessel indicating imperial power, the Empire 具 ¹¹⁴ (鼎). It is said that the great Yu (King and founder of the first dynasty, the Xia), collected all the metalware from nine states and made them into nine three-legged *"Ding"* 具 (鼎).¹¹⁵

This radical should be compared with *precious* 𣆪 (貝, R. 154); with *origin* 𦣻 (自, R. 132); and with *the first* 鼻 (鼻, R. 209). All of these suggest the *original, precious, first* couple. The symbols indicating the first couple are ⋀ , △△ , and = . The "feet" of the figure 具 represent God's *hands* 八 .

A *tripod with small opening in the top* 鼐 ¹¹⁶ (鼐) reveals God 丨 (⼘ , R. 25) surmounting the vessel.

Radical 209 (225)

Oracle Bone   Bronzeware   Traditional   Simplified

Definition: before any others, the first, the nose

Analysis: The interrelationship among many radicals is most interesting. This present radical *before any others, the first* 鼻 ¹¹⁷ is clearly related to *precious* 𣆪 (貝 , R. 154) and *origin* 𦣻 (自 , R. 132). The several modern interpretations are defined relative to "the nose." In 鼻 we find *original, source* 𦣻 (自 , R. 132); God's *hands* 𦥑 (臼 , R. 134) enclosing and forming the *noble* 大 (大 , R. 37) person as 夬 , while a second *noble* 大 (大) person looks on. The radical 鼻 (鼻) therefore well portrays the meaning *before any others, first,* in depicting the first couple.

As to a possible "nose connection"—the "first life" came to Adam when *"the LORD God . . . breathed into his <u>nostrils</u> the breath of life; and man became a living being. (Genesis 2: 7).*

Radical 108 (146)

| Oracle Bone | Bronzeware | Traditional | Simplified |

Definition: vessel. utensil

Analysis: In the Hebrew Scriptures, man is often called a "vessel," and God the "Potter."

> Yet, O Lord, You are our Father. We are the clay. You are the potter; we are all the work of your hand. (Isaiah 64: 8, NIV).

From foregoing radicals (R. 121, R. 193, R. 98), we learned that the Chinese had the same concept of God as a Potter:

Your sovereign goodness cannot be measured. As a potter, You have made all living things.[118]

The oracle bone radical, *vessel, utensil* [119] (皿) portrays two conjoined, back-to-back *persons* (人) from *clay, earth* (土 , R. 32). The bronzeware figure [120] (皿) depicts two back-to-back *persons* from the ground —.

two person + clay = vessel

God planned to use Adam and his wife to show forth His love and glory. In the character *benefit, advantage* [121] (益), we see the *vessel* and the *water* (水) of life that God gave the first couple to drink, to *benefit* them with everlasting life, (See next Section).

Radical 151 (191)

| Oracle Bone | Bronzeware | Traditional 豆 | Simplified 豆 |

Beginnings—Creation

Definition: a bronze vessel for sacrifice, beans

Analysis: In the oracle bone version of *vessel of bronze for sacrifice* 豆 122 (豆), we again see Adam and his wife portrayed as vessels.

△ + ▽ + = = 豆

dust　　person　　two　　　　vessel for sacrifice

The character *abundant, fruitful* 豐 123 (豐) clearly indicates that the couple, the *vessels* 豆 (豆), were created by the three members of the Godhead 彐 + ヒ + 丫 (see R. 113 and 101). They were created to be *fruitful*, as the Hebrew Scriptures record:

> Then God blessed them, and God said to them, "Be fruitful and multiply; (Genesis 1: 28).

豆　　+　彐 + 丫 + ヒ　　=　豐

vessel (the couple)　　*The Godhead*　　*fruitful, abundant*

Radical 207 (223)　鼓　　鼓　鼓

Oracle Bone　Bronzeware　Traditional　Simplified

Definition: to raise, stir up, a drum

Analysis: *To raise, stir up* 鼓, 鼓 124 (鼓) can be compared with *abundant* 豐 (豐, see under R. 151). Again it is clear that Adam and his wife, the first two *vessels* 豆 (豆, R. 151), were *created* 生 (生, R. 100) by the three Persons of the Godhead: 丫 (甫, see R. 101); 彐 (又, R. 29); and ↑ (矢, R. 111). They were given the breath of life by the Holy

89

Spirit, represented by ↑, that *raised* 壴𠃜 (鼓) them to life.

壴 + Ψ, ʔ, ↑ = 壴𠃜

vessel   *Godhead*   *raise, stir up*

The bronzeware graph 壴𠃜 is identical except that the symbol Ψ for God is replaced by 大, God with upraised arms.

In *longevity* 彭 [125] (彭), "God's presence" 彡 (彡, R. 59) can be seen. The first couple could enjoy *longevity* as long as they ate of the tree of life.

Radical 137 (182)   △   Ⅲ   舟   舟

Oracle Bone Bronzeware Traditional Simplified

Definition: vessel, boat, ["person(s)"]

Analysis: Because of its use in many characters, this radical has proven to be a real challenge! Was it the original intention of the inventor of Chinese characters that this symbol represent a vessel as "person(s)," or a "boat?" The bronzeware for *boat, vessel* 舟口 [126] (船) has been interpreted as a *vessel* 舟 (舟) for *eight* 八 (八) *persons* 口 (口), representing the very first boat. Noah, his wife, his three sons and their wives (making eight persons), escaped the worldwide flood in the ark. (Genesis 6-8). (See p. ix, "Historical Perspectives").

But why, in the contemporary character 舟 are there two *"flames of fire"* ∶ (R. 3)? This symbol • has usually been reserved for holy person(s), for example: 交 (交 . see R. 67 for full explanation, p. 44). Could it be that the original representation was of "person(s)," but with usage, in time, the radical's meaning changed to "boat?" Let us consider this as we examine oracle bone and bronzeware graphs of *vessel* 𠙵 , ◇ [127] 皿 , 𠙹 [128] (舟).

To begin with, we should compare one oracle bone rendition of *breath* 𠙵 (風 , R. 182), which appears to be identical with *vessel* 𠙵 (舟). Next, let us examine the character *sort, kind* 𠙶 , 𠙷 [129] 𠙸 [130] (般). On the fifth and sixth days of the creation week, God had created all *sorts* of animals, "*each according to its kind,*" (Genesis 1: 21, 24), and Adam had given each its name. But although every animal had a mate, Adam had none. "*And the LORD God said, 'It is not good that man should be alone; I will make him a helper comparable to him.*" (Genesis 2: 18). So, after putting Adam to sleep, God took one of his ribs and made his mate. When Adam awoke, he said: ". . .*She shall be called Woman, because she was taken out of Man.*" (Genesis 2:23).

If 𠙵 in the oracle bone symbol is the *vessel*—Adam, then from him, we find a *person* ○ (口); ⊐ (人) emerging in 𠙶 and 𠙷 , one after his own *kind, sort* (般). In 𠙸 we also find a second *person* □ (丁), the woman. The characters 般配 used together mean *perfect matching mates,* or *matching perfectly.*

If 𠙵 were truly a boat, why would it always be represented as standing on end? However, if 𠙵 represents two persons, we may find them standing as ⌐ + ¬ , with outstretched arms.

When *vessel* is written as 夂 , we can see two back-to-back, bowing figures as 丆 + 𠃊 . In the character *before, in front of* 𠨉 [131] (前), the couple appear to be ascending a mountain where God is standing (see R. 25). Note also *respectful, quiet* 𠊱 [132] (俞). In both of these character transcriptions, the *vessel* 舟 has been replaced by *flesh* 月 , a radical also indicating the first couple (see R. 130).

A significant character in which we find the *vessel* 𠙵 is *to begin, initiate* 𦥑𠙵 , 𦥑𠙵 (興 , see the next radical, R. 134 for full explanation).

Let us also examine *to create* 𦥯[133] (造). If 舟 represents a boat, why would 告 meaning *to speak*, and containing 生 (生 , R. 100) *to bring forth life* be used?

Finally, it is interesting to find how 臼 metamorphosed into in the contemporary writing. In the *Shou Wen* R. 309 writing, it becomes 舟 [134], where the back-to-back persons 𠂉 + 𠃉 are even more clearly seen. The next step appears to be 舟 [135] (舟). In this seal figure, we find, for the first time, the two *"flames of fire"* ∶ . In the seal writing, one commonly-written form of *person* 亻 (人) is 阝 (𠂆 , with head added). In 阝, we find the calligrapher has made two persons by drawing the horizontal line through it, as 舟 , in addition to adding the two *"flames of fire"* ∶ , indicating *two holy persons* 舟 (舟), or *vessels*.

Radical 134 (179)

Seal	Traditional	Simplified
臼	臼	臼

Definition: to hold in both hands, to reveal, a bowl

Analysis: This radical appears to have been written two ways: first, with hands locked as in 臼[136] (臼). The second way of writing the radical is with God's hands separated. *To begin initiate, establish, found* 興 , 興 , 興[137] (興) shows the creation of mankind. The symbols 臼 and 臼 are *vessels* (舟 , see discussion under R. 137), and represent person(s). Adam 臼 is in God's hands 𦥑 , and 凵 represents the creation of the woman, as seen in *to begin, initiate, found* 興 (興). In 興 both *"vessels"* are depicted in the one symbol 臼 , with the addition of the *perfect* 丨 person, woman, to the *vessel* 臼 , representing Adam.

Beginnings—Creation

Radical 174 (202)

凸	凸	青	青
Oracle Bone	Bronzeware	Traditional	Simplified

Definition: young, grow, produce, color of nature

Analysis: This radical, *grow, produce, young* 凸 ¹³⁸ 凸 ¹³⁹ (青) is most interesting. In the bronzeware figure ⚇ (生 . R. 100), we recognize *to beget, bring forth life*. Does the symbol 日 indicate a holy *vessel* 日 (舟 , R. 137), person? Actually, the figure 日 ¹⁴⁰ (丹), means *to confer long life, red*. This would be logical, for since Adam, the *vessel* 日 , was created in God's image, and the name, Adam, denotes "red." He was given *conditional* "immortality" 日 , as long as he obeyed and was loyal to God, especially as he refrained from eating of the forbidden tree of the knowledge of good and evil. Immortality would, of course, also give eternal youth!

日 + ⚇ = 凸

immortality   *life*   *youthful*

In the bronzeware character *quiet, peaceful, clean* ⚇ ¹⁴¹ (静), we again find the *youthful* 凸 (青) Adam, but the Creator's *hand* ∏ (爪 , R. 87) and His *powerful, strong* ⌇ (力 , R. 19) right arm are also seen as an object of worship with uplifted *hand* ⌇ (扌 , R. 64).

凸 + ∏ + ⌇ + ⌇ = ⚇

youthful *God's hand* *strong* *hand* *quiet, peaceful*

Radical 96 (88, 131)

王		玉	玉
Oracle Bone	Bronzeware	Traditional	Simplified

Definition: gem, precious stone (especially jade), valuable

Analysis: From the radical 丰, 王 ¹⁴² (玉), meaning *gem, precious stone, valuable,* we learn how Adam, the *perfect* | (十, R. 24) person was *valuable,* like *a precious gem* 丰 to God the Father Ψ (see under R. 101), and to all *three* ☰ (三) Members of the Godhead.

Of interest is the fact that both oracle bone and bronzeware versions of *king, ruler* are also written as 王 ¹⁴³ (王). *King, ruler* can also be written as 立, which is similar to 立 (立, R. 117), meaning *to create, establish, stand up*— a graph showing Adam standing in God's presence. Adam, who was *precious* 丰, 王 (玉) in God's eyes was given the position of *ruler* 立 (王) over the earth. The Hebrew record relates:

> Then God said, 'Let us make man in our image and likeness to <u>rule</u> the fish in the sea, the birds of heaven, the cattle, all wild animals on earth, and all reptiles that crawl upon the earth.' (Genesis 1: 26, NEB).

|	+	☰	=	王
Perfect (Adam)		three (Godhead)		ruler, king

Radical 167 (208)   𡈼   金   金

Oracle Bone   Bronzeware   Traditional   Simplified

Definition: gold, precious, money, metal, durable

Analysis: Another radical with the meaning of *precious* is *gold* 金, 金 ¹⁴⁴ (金). There is no oracle bone version of this radical, but in the bronzeware, we see Adam, the *ruler* 王, 立 (王, R. 96). God's *mouth* ⌂ (upside down ㄩ) speaks from heaven, giving the mandate to Adam and his wife, indicated by the number *two* ＝ (二, R. 7) to be the *rulers*

Beginnings—Creation

王. In the second version of *gold, precious* 金, we find the *ruler* 土 (王, see R. 96) identified as the *great* 大 (大, R. 37) person standing before God's presence.

To *mold, make, cast (metals)* 鑄 [145] (鑄) has the figure 冃, reminiscent of *a large earthen pot* 鬲 (鬲, R. 193), showing God's hands 𠂇𠂆 molding the *metal* 金 (金). In the graph, we find a *river* 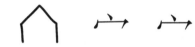 and two *persons* 廾, indicating the River of Life. It was God's intention that the precious first couple live forever!

Radical 40 (45)

⌂ ⌐ ⌐

Oracle Bone   Bronzeware   Traditional   Simplified

Definition: a roof

Analysis: The characters for *roof* ⌂ [146] (宀) and the number *six* ⌂⌂ [147] (六) both portray a house, but the latter has eves on the house. Why should the number *six* be depicted as a house or home? The Hebrew Scriptures relate that on the *sixth* day of creation, the first home was established.

> *So God created man in His own image: in the image of God He created him; male and female He created them. . .So the evening and the morning were the <u>sixth day</u>.*
> *(Genesis 1: 27, 31.)*

But the week consists of seven days. We read again:

> *Thus the heavens and the earth, and all the host of them, were finished. And on the <u>seventh day</u> God ended His work which He had done, and He <u>rested</u> on the seventh day from all His work which He had done. Then God blessed the <u>seventh day</u> and sanctified it, because in it He <u>rested</u> from all His work which God had created and made.   (Genesis 2: 1-3).*

How interesting that the character *to rest in, private dwelling* 宀 ¹⁴⁸ (宅) shows a *home* 宀 with the number *seven* 丅 ¹⁴⁹ (七)! On the seventh day God rested after establishing the first *home* on the *sixth* day.

The first couple's *religion* 宗 ¹⁵⁰ (宗) was founded on the *perfect* ∣ (十) Person from *above* 二 (丅 , see R. 113), who was Lord of their *home* 宀 (宀). They were to *follow* Him and *honor* Him.

∣ + 二 = 丅 + 宀 = 宗

perfect   above   "God radical"   home   religion
(Person)   follow, honor

And so, Adam and his wife, the first two *persons* □ + □ ¹⁵¹(丁), cleverly united as 中 , could describe their beautiful garden of Eden *home* 宀 (宀) as a *palace* 宮 ¹⁵² (宮).

There is much to learn regarding this ancient, special Garden of Eden that a loving God prepared for the first man and woman, Adam and his wife. We shall next study, in Section III, that in the garden was a Holy Mountain, where the first couple daily worshiped God. Their devotion to the Creator is well portrayed by the venerable Chinese in the clever pictographic radicals—the basic elements of their writing.

---

¹ Chung-kuo k'e-hsueh-yuan k'ao-ku yen-chiu-so, *Chia-Ku Wen-Pien* (Peking: K'ao-ku-hsueh chuan-k'an yi-chung ti-shih-ssu hao, 1965), no. 6.8, [Hereafter abbreviated CKWP].

² CKWP, no. 2.6.

³ *The Works of Motze*, p. 240

4 CKWP, no. 1.9.
5 Hung pei Chiang, *Ching Wen P'ien Ching Wen* (Taipei: Kung I Publ. Co., 1974), no. 1.13. [Hereafter abbreviated HPC].
6 Ibid.
7 Ma Wei Ching, *Wei Ching Chia Ku Wen Yuan* (Yunlin: Ma Fu Distributor, 1971), p. 1409, [Hereafter abbreviated MWC].
8 HPC, no. 1.16.
9 Ibid.
10 CKWP, no, 7,15.
11 HPC, no. 7.22.
12 Ibid..
13 CKWP, no. 7.16.
14 MWC, p. 179.
15 W.M. Hawley, *Oriental Culture Chart # 6 (Chinese Seal Characters).* [Hereafter abbreviated Hawley].
16 CKWP, no. 5.24.
17 HPC, no, 5.37.
18 Ibid.
19 Jia Gu Wen, *Zi Shuo Li* (Taiwan: An Guo Jun, 1993), p. 63. [Hereafter abbreviated JGW].
20 Hawley.
21 HPC, no. 7.22.
22 Ibid.
23 CKWP, no. 11.14.
24 HPC, no. 11.10.
25 Ibid.
26 CKWP, no. 13.4.
27 MWC, p. 330.
28 Hawley.
29 MWC, p. 334.
30 Hawley.
31 CKWP, no. 4.16.
32 HPC, no. 4.14.
33 Ibid.
34 CKWP, no. 5.10.
35 HPC, no. 5.17.
36 Ibid.
37 CKWP, No. 10.5.
38 HPC, no. 10.3.
39 Ibid.
40 CKWP, no. 10.3.
41 HPC, no. 10.3.

42 Ibid.
43 CKWP, no. 10.1.
44 HPC, no. 10.1.
45 Ibid.
46 CKWP, no. 9.9.
47 HPC, no. 9.18.
48 Ibid.
49 MWC, p. 299.
50 Hawley.
51 CKWP, no. 10.11.
52 Gia Fu Feng and Jane English, *Translation of Lao Zi, Tao Te Ching* (Toronto: Vintage Books, Random House, Inc., 1989), Ch. 25, p. 27.
53 Ibid., no. 8.1.
54 Ibid., no. 1.1.
55 Ma Wei Ching, *Wei Ching Chia Ku Wen Yuan* (Yunlin: Ma Fu Distributor, 1971), p. 383. [Hereafter abbreviated MWC].
56 CKWP, no. 12.14.
57 Ibid., no. 13.7.
58 Ibid. no. 8.8.
59 Jia Gu Wen, *Zi Shuo Li* (Taiwan: An Guo Jun, 1983), p. 6..
60 CKWP, no. 5.2.
61 MWC, p. 1297; HPC, no, 5.9.
62 CKWP, no. 10.16.
63 Kang Xi Dictionary (Taipei: Da Shen Publ., 1978), *I Jing:* p. 153.
64 CKWP, no. 14.15.
65 MWC, p. 549.
66 Ibid., p. 357.
67 CKWP, no, 3.10.
68 MWC, p. 551.
69 HPC, no. 14.29.
70 Ibid., no, 7.1.
71 Lin Chih Ch'ing, *Ting Cheng Liu Shu T'ung* (Shanghai: Kuang I Publ. Co., 1936), Sn. 1, part vii, p. 17. [Hereafter abbreviated LCC].
72 CKWP, no. 7.3.
73 Ibid. no. 7.2.
74 Ibid., no. 12.2.
75 Ibid., no. 13.6.
76 Ibid., no. 12.2.
77 Ibid., no. 7.7.
78 Ibid., no. 7.8.
79 Ibid., no. 7.6.
80 Ibid., no. 4.22.

[81] LCC, Sn. 1, part viii, p. 33 under
[82] CKWP, no. 5.18.
[83] Ibid.
[84] MWC, p. 795.
[85] CKWP, no. 12.4.
[86] Ibid., no. 12.10.
[87] Ibid., no. 7.16.
[88] Ibid.
[89] Ibid., no. 12.6.
[90] Ibid., no. 1.10.
[91] Ibid. 8.7.; HPC , no. 8.10.
[92] Ibid., no. 10.17.
[93] Wu Shuping, Lai Chang-yang, *The Four Books and Five Jing in Modern Chinese, Vol. 4* (Beijing: International Culture Publication, Inc., 1996), *Li Ki*, p. 722.
[94] CKWP, no, 9,2.
[95] Ibid., no. 9.4.
[96] Ibid., no. 9.2.
[97] HPC, no. 9.9.
[98] MWC, p. 1081.
[99] HPC, no. 4.15.
[100] Ibid., no. 3.3.
[101] Ibid. , p. 1090.
[102] Ibid., p. 552.
[103] CKWP, no. 10,11.
[104] Ibid., no. 10.9.
[105] Ibid., no. 5.19.
[106] HPC, no. 5.10.
[107] HPC, no. 5.30.
[108] Ibid., no. 1.12.
[109] CKWP, no. 3.9.
[110] HPC, no. 3.16.
[111] Ibid., no. 3.17.
[112] MWC, p. 990.
[113] Ibid., SN. 6, p. 17.
[114] HPC, no. 7.15.
[115] Ciyuan, *Etiology of Chinese Characters* (Beijing: The Commercial Press, 1979), p. 1954.
[116] Ibid., no. 7.16.
[117] Ibid., no. 6.26.
[118] James Legge, *The Notions of the Chinese Concerning God and Spirits* (Hong Kong: Hong Kong Register Office, 1852), p. 30.

[119] CKWP, no. 5.11.
[120] HPC, no. 5.19.
[121] MWC, p. 1134.
[122] CKWP, no. 5.9.
[123] Ibid., no. 5.10.
[124] CKWP, no. 5.8.
[125] I bid.
[126] HPC, no. 8.21.
[127] CKWP, no. 8.10.
[128] HPC, no. 8.21.
[129] MWC, p. 1129.
[130] Ibid., p. 1130
[131] HPC, vol. ii, p. 1010.
[132] HPC, no. 8.21.
[133] HPC, no. 2.21).
[134] LCC, Sn. 3, p. 33.
[135] Ibid., Sn. 3, p. 2.
[136] Ibid., Sn. II, Part 7, p. 10.
[137] MWC, pp. 624, 625.
[138] Ibid., p. 113.
[139] HPC, no. 5.23.
[140] CKWP, no. 5.14.
[141] HPC, no. 5.23.
[142] MWC, p. 91.
[143] CKWP, no. 1.8.
[144] HPC, no. 14.1.
[145] Ibid., no. 14.2.
[146] Ibid., no. 7.17.
[147] Ibid., no. 14.7.
[148] Ibid., no. 7..17.
[149] Ibid., no. 14.8.
[150] Ibid., no. 7.19.
[151] Ibid., no. 14.12.
[152] Ibid., no., 7.23.

Section III

BEGINNINGS—
WORSHIP OF GOD

 (首)

**A glorious high throne from
the beginning
Is the place of our sanctuary.
(Jeremiah 17: 12)**

Beginnings—Worship of God

Section II revealed that, according to both the Chinese and Hebrew record, the first home of Adam and Eve was a beautiful Garden of Eden. Furthermore, it appears that the garden had a central Holy Mountain (or perhaps the whole garden composed the mountain!)

The Bible is plentifully supplied with references to "My Holy Hill." For a better understanding of the significance of such a site in both the Old and New Testaments, see Appendix I.

The Hebrew Scriptures do record that *"they [Adam and his wife] heard the sound of the LORD God walking in the garden in the cool of the day." (Genesis 3: 8)*. So it seems that God made frequent, if not daily, visits with His newly created human friends.

This present section portrays the ancient worship of God by the first couple on the Holy Mount. Because they were holy and sinless, having been created in God's image, Adam and his wife were able to meet with God face-to-face as He descended upon the Holy Mountain. All of this is portrayed by the ancient Chinese linguistic artists who seemingly hurried about like busy photographers documenting pictographically every detail of the original home and the first sanctuary-temple of mankind.

The Beginning of Chinese Characters

Radical 102 (142)

田　　田　　田　　田

Oracle bone　Bronzeware　Traditional　Simplified

Definition: field, landed property, garden

Analysis: The beautiful *garden* 田 ¹ (田) that God prepared for Adam and Eve was called Eden.

> *Now a river went out of Eden to water the garden,*
> *And from there it parted and became four riverheads.*
> *(Genesis 2:10)*

The radical 田 is a perfect topographical depiction of the garden with the river arising in the center of the garden, and its four diverging branches ⊕.

Adam was given the garden, according to the character *male, baron* 田 ² (甸). Here we find the *strong* ∕ (力, R. 19) right arm of God presenting the *garden* 田. A baron is a nobleman who receives land from a king. Furthermore, Adam, the baron, was to *cultivate* 田 ³ (畈) the garden, as the *Father* (父, R. 88) commanded him.

In addition, Adam, the first *man* (人, R. 9), was given the Garden of Eden as his *imperial domain* 田 ⁴ (甸) to rule over it as a baron, under God, his King.

Radical 20(26)

勹　　勹　　勹

Oracle bone　Bronzeware　Traditional　Simplified

Definition: to wrap, enfold, include

Analysis: A pictogram of God Ｙ , ⼈ , Ｙ enfolding various objects is seen in this character, *to wrap, enfold* 勹 , 勹 , 勹 ⁵ (勹).

In *to hold, surround* 🗚 6 (包), God enfolds *man* 𠂉 (人). In *equal, even* 𠃌 7 (勻), He holds *two* 二 (二 , R. 7) persons, Adam and his wife, who are of *equal* worth.

To grasp with both hands, a double handful 𠂇 8 (掬) depicts the *perfect* | (十 , R. 24) man lying horizontal between the creating hands 𠂇 of God who *enfolds* him.

The character 甫 (甫 , under R. 101), we found, has several meanings: *Father, garden,* and *beginning.* In the *beginning* 甫 , Adam and his wife, *fell prostrate* 𠂉 9 (匍) before God ⺈ (勹) who *enfolded* them. They were perfectly devoted to serving their loving God who had given them their beautiful garden home. The *garden* 田 (田 , R. 102) was originally God's *imperial domain* 甸 10 (甸), but He had presented it to Adam to "tend and keep." (Genesis 2: 15).

Radical 201 寅 黃 黃

Oracle bone Bronzeware Traditional Simplified

Definition: yellow, imperial color

Analysis: Who is this imposing *noble* 大 (大 , R. 37) man upon whom the *garden* 田 (田 , R. 102) is superimposed in the pictogram, *yellow, imperial color* 寅 11 黃 12, 黃 13 (黃)? It must refer to Adam, the first man on earth who was made in God's sun-like, bright image.

An oracle bone character meaning *authority* 𠂉 14 (衡) further confirms that this radical 寅 is Adam, for he is being given authority over the garden by the *Father* 父 (父). We learn further that the dominion given him was the Holy Mountain. This mountain-garden in its pristine beauty— *uncultivated, great, extensive* 荒 15 (荒) gave Adam great responsibility. The *"yellow" noble man* 黃 is found on the *mountain* 山 (山 ,

R. 46). Regarding the duty to *"tend and keep,"* *(Genesis 2: 15)* the garden, an ancient Chinese poem states:

> **Tian [Heaven, God] made a high mountain [山]**
> **The great king cultivated [荒] it.**[16]

The "great king" could well apply to Adam, the *"yellow"* 黃 (黄) man who mirrored God's shining glory!

Radical 46 (60)

Oracle bone   Bronzeware   Traditional   Simplified

Definition: mountain, hill, range of mountains, island

Analysis: This is a very important radical, for it becomes apparent that a mountain in Eden was the site of worship and communion with God for the first couple. This *mountain* always has three peaks in the various pictograms: 〰,〰,〰,[17] ▲ [18] (山) in the oracle bone and bronzeware. This must have been a holy place, for we see the "blackening" of the bronzeware figure ▲ . According to Jeremiah 17: 12, *"in the beginning,"* God located His sanctuary on a "high" place:

> *A glorious high throne from*
> *the beginning*
> *Is the place of our sanctuary.*

Note also that this was a *"glorious"* place. How significant that the Chinese have forms of *fire* 〰, 〰 (火, R. 86) that are similar to *mountain!* Examine now a character meaning *burning* 〰[19] (焚). This shows not only the mountain, but also the two special *trees* 林 (木, R. 75). Evidently these trees were located on top of the mountain, in the very center of the garden.

And out of the ground the LORD God made every tree grow that is

Beginnings—Worship of God

pleasant to the sight and good for food. The tree of life was also in the midst of the garden, and the tree of the knowledge of good and evil. (Genesis 2:9).

An additional character, *mountain, large rock* 山 [20] (岙) shows the three *Persons* ㅂㅂ (口, R. 30) of the Godhead, further suggesting that the *mountain* 山 was holy.

Radical 210

𐎠𐎠   𐎡   齊   齐

Oracle bone Bronzeware Traditional Simplified

Definition: all alike, equal, respect, pious, chaste

Analysis: 𐎠𐎠 + 𐎱 = 𐎡

Three Persons   mountain   all alike, equal

The oracle bone rendition of *all alike, equal, pious* 𐎠𐎠 [21] (齊) reveals the three Persons of the Godhead, especially suggested by the YYY configuration (see R. 1). Note that in the bronzeware, however, their location on the Holy Mount 𐎱 (山 , R. 46) is evident in 𐎡 [22] (齊) where it appears that the first couple are also present as ⊃ (persons made in the image of *Heaven, God* 大 [23] [天 , R.(90)]. Compare *all alike, equal* 𐎡 (齊) with the previous character discussed under R. 46, *mountain, large rock* 山 (岙).

That this radical 𐎡 refers to the Godhead is further suggested by the character *pure, refined, to fast* 示𐎠𐎠 [24] (齋) where 𐎠𐎠 is combined with the "God radical," 示 (R. 113).

Radical 27 (22)

┌   ⟨⟩   ┌   ┌

Oracle bone Bronzeware Traditional Simplified

Definition: hill, cliff

Analysis: It may come as a surprise that the Holy Mountain of Eden is so important that the Chinese have about 45 radicals related to this subject! The mountain takes many forms, but can easily be identified. In *hill, cliff* ┌ 25 ⟨⟩ 26 (厂), we have several observations.

First, please note the bronzeware ⟨⟩ and ⟨⟩. This hill is identified as belonging to the Great Unity ⟨⟩ (一, R. 1), symbolized by the *Shield* ⟨⟩ (干, R. 51), a metaphor for Jesus Christ, or the Godhead.

Second, why should the oracle bone ┌ have this configuration? Recall the character *to command* ⟨⟩ (⟨⟩, under R. 26). Here was pictured the *command, mandate* to Adam, depicted as ⟨⟩, from God's *mouth* △. We again find God's creative mouth in ┌, but this time pictorially oriented as the mountain.

Next we must examine the character *beginning, source, origin* ⟨⟩ 27 (原). How interesting that the "beginning and origin" occurred on the Holy Hill in the Garden of Eden. Note the three dots ⟨⟩ on the *Fountain* ⟨⟩ (泉). The Shuo Wen character ⟨⟩ 28 (原) has the "God" radical ⟨⟩ superimposed on three Fountains. The Godhead is the "Fountain of Life."

> And He said to me, "It is done! I am the Alpha and the Omega, the Beginning and the End. I will give of the <u>fountain of the water of life</u> freely to him who thirsts. (Revelation 21: 6).

Radical 170 (33)

Oracle bone　Bronzeware　Traditional　Simplified

Definition: mound, hill

Analysis: It becomes apparent that this *hill, mound* 29 (阝, 阜) is a holy hill. In the bronzeware forms 30, we find three "holy" Persons. Also note that actually consists of three ⌐ (⌐ , R. 27), or three *mouths* (口 , R. 30) of the Godhead. The conclusion is that the Holy Mount is visited by God and is His Holy Hill.

God is represented by the Chinese as *descending* 31 (降) to the Holy Hill of Eden. The graph 32 (止) depict His feet descending. In the bronzeware, *descending* 33 (降), both the hill and the feet are "blackened," indicating holiness.

In the character *mound, tumulus* 34 (陵), we find the *noble* (大) Person, who has descended, *to stop* (止) on the Holy *Hill* . So it appears that Tian [Heaven, God] has descended to meet with the first couple, and commune with them there. That the in represents Tian [Heaven, God] and not Adam is confirmed by another oracle bone graph of *mound, tumulus* 35 (陵) where Adam is represented by an uplifted, worshiping hand .

Radical 61 (81)

Oracle bone　Bronzeware　Traditional　Simplified

Definition: heart, mind, affections, intention

Analysis: The bronzeware and Shuo Wen graphs of *heart, mind* ,

109

The Beginning of Chinese Characters

⸜ʋ⸝ ³⁶ (心) portray two conjoined worshiping persons ⸜ + ⸝ (⸜ʋ⸝ , adding "heads"), with the second person emerging from the first, even as the woman came from Adam's side. Furthermore, note the black dot • (﹑, R. 3), indicating holiness, on the bronzeware form ⸜ʋ⸝ . Originally, their relationship with God was intimate as a *Father* 田 (甫 , under R. 101) with His children. God delighted to bestow His *favor, kindness, benevolence* ³⁷ (惠) upon the *person* ○ (厶 , R. 28)—Adam or his wife, whose *heart* ⸜ʋ⸝ (心) was turned toward Him.

田   +   ○   +   ⸜ʋ⸝   =   惠

Father (God)   *person*   *heart*   *favor, kindness*

The character *exert the mind, make an effort* ³⁸ (懋) shows Adam, the man of *dust* (土 , R. 32) using his *mind* ⸜ʋ⸝ (心) concerning God's command not to eat from the *tree* (木 , R. 75) of the knowledge of good and evil (which stood next to the tree of life). A second character regarding God's specific *command* (令 , under R. 26) is *to think, recall, remember* ³⁹ (念). Here we find God's *mouth* △ (口 , R. 30) advising the first couple to use the *mind, heart* ⸜ʋ⸝ (心) to remember His one and only command. In this character ⸜ʋ⸝ the *hands* of the worshipers that form the *heart* ⸜ʋ⸝ are clearly seen.

Radical 161 (187)   內   㢫   辰   辰

Oracle bone   Bronzeware   Traditional   Simplified

Definition: early morning, 7-9 a.m.

Analysis: Here is a radical that tells us when the first couple went to the Holy Mount to worship God. In the *early morning* ⁴⁰ ⁴¹ (辰) we find the place of worship, the *hill* (厂 , R. 27). The couple

110

Beginnings—Worship of God

are represented by a *perfect* | (十, R. 24) person with two ╱ arms outstretched. In 帀 we find two persons ⊔ᴎ.

At *daybreak* 晨⁴² (晨), God receives them with open arms (*hands*) ⋏⋏. The site of their worship is further portrayed in 林 ⁴³ 林⁴⁴ (農), today meaning *farming, agriculture,* but originally indicating the middle of the Garden of Eden where the two special *trees* 木木 (木, R. 75) were located. God had given them their work to cultivate and keep the garden.

Radical 115 (149)   禾   禾   禾   禾
Oracle bone Bronzeware Traditional Simplified

Definition: growing grain, crops

Analysis: From the appearance of the ancient forms of *growing grain, crops* 禾 ⁴⁵ 禾⁴⁶(禾), we might speculate that the "grain" is symbolic of a *Person* 人 (人, R. 9), a holy Person, from the "blackening" of ◆ (丶, R. 3). From this usage, it would appear that *Grain* represents God. In the Hebrew language, *"bar"* means not only *grain, wheat, corn,* but also *son, pure, clear.* Therefore, it would seem that this *Person* 人, *Grain* 禾 would most likely represent the <u>Son</u> of God, Jesus Christ. In fact, Jesus referred to Himself as "a grain of wheat" as He related this symbolism in reference to His sacrificial death with consequent redemption of believing mankind:

> "Most assuredly, I say to you, unless <u>a grain of wheat</u> falls into the ground and dies, it remains alone; but if it dies, it produces much grain." (John 12:24)

The character *majestic, profound* 穆 ⁴⁷ (穆) reveals the glory of the Godhead in the *Sun* ☉ (日, R. 72), the three *Perfect* 川 (十, R. 24) Persons of the Godhead, and "God's presence" ⫽ (彡, R. 59).

In Psalm 24: 3, 4, we read:

> *Who may ascend into the hill of the Lord*
> *Or who may stand in His holy place?*
> *He who has clean hands and a pure ["bar"] heart.*

In the character *to report to the throne* 🈳 48 (秦), we find the three Persons of the Godhead 人 , 人 , 人 at the site of the two *trees* 林 (木 , R. 75), and the worshiping *hands* 𠂉 of the first couple.

Radical 214

Oracle bone   Bronzeware   Traditional   Simplified

Definition: a flute, tube

Analysis: The oracle bone renderings of a *flute* 49 50 (龠) reveal differently depicted *mouths* ⌒ , △ (口 , R. 30) for "blowing the flute." In there are two holy persons (see R. 3 and R. 24), apparently the first couple. In , however, the *mouth* △ forms not only the Holy Mountain, but appears to be God's mouth (compare under R. 26). The three Persons of the Godhead are portrayed as . The figure ▭ represents God's *breath* (風 , R. 182). So we find not only Adam and his wife, but also the Godhead taking part in making music in this holy place.

The character *harmony, peaceful, be on good terms* 51(龢) contains God's *mouth* △ ; the *mouths* and *breaths* of the first couple; and the overspreading symbol 木 representing the Son of God (the *wheat* 木 , see discussion under the previous R. 115). How much significance the ancient Chinese calligrapher put into one small pictogram!

Beginnings—Worship of God

Radical 34

㠯　　𠂉　　夂

Oracle bone　Bronzeware　Traditional　Simplified

Definition: to follow

Analysis: Although this radical is the primary radical in only a few characters, it is found as a constituent in a number of characters. The question is: does this radical *to follow* 𠂉 52　㠯 53 (夂) refer to God or man? We believe that it may refer to either, depending upon the context of the characters. The original pictograms appear to be that of a foot. Let us first examine *to descend from heaven* 𨺉 54 (降), where there is no doubt that these are God's feet 𠂆 descending. The feet are descending to the holy *mount* ⻖ (阝 , R. 170).

In the character *suddenly, hastily* 條 55 (條), we find God's foot coming down to the *tree* 朩 (木 , R. 75). This most likely refers to one of the special trees located on the top of the central peak of the Holy Mountain.

A beautiful seal character that we have not found in either the oracle bone or bronzeware, nevertheless should be shown, *love, affection* 㤅 56 (愛). Here, on the holy *hill* 厂 (厂 , R. 27), the first couple, conjoined as the *heart, mind* 心 (心 , R. 61), are worshiping God's descended feet, depicted as 屮 and 㝆. (The *Shuo Wen* pictogram resembles a person 几). This character portrays the *love and affection* 㤅 of God for the first couple as He descends to be with them on the Holy Mountain.

Radical 147 (107)

目　　　　見　见

Oracle bone　Bronzeware　Traditional　Simplified

Definition: to see, visit, face to face, examine

Analysis: This radical, *to see, visit* 𥃩 , 𥄎 ⁵⁷(見) reveals the man 𠄌 , 𠂉 (卩 , R. 26; 人, R. 9), Adam visiting eye-to-eye with the "all-Seeing-*Eye*" 𠃬 (目 , R. 109), God. Their visit must, therefore, have taken place on the Holy *Hill* 厂 (厂 , R. 27). This character *to see, visit* 𥃩 (見) is similar to the radical, *the head* 𩑋 (頁 , R. 181), as both concern the man 𠄌 . However, this latter radical depicts Adam's creation, rather his visiting God.

Radical 14 (18)

∩   冖   冖

Oracle bone Bronzeware Traditional Simplified

Definition: a cover (mountain)

Analysis: Although one meaning of the radical is *cover* ∩ ⁵⁸ (冖), a better definition is "mountain." This becomes evident when examining the character *peak, mound, highest, summit* 𩎖 ⁵⁹(冢) where the figure meaning *to see, visit* 𥄎 (見 , R. 147) is found. The character therefore tells us that to see or visit with God, the first man had to go to the Holy Mountain. The *Shuo Wen* character 𩓣 ⁶⁰ (冢) also shows an *eye* ⊖ (目 , R. 109), as well as a *person* 𠆢 (儿 , R. 10).

Radical 64 (111)

ᗩ   ⼿   ⼿   ⼿

Oracle bone Bronzeware Traditional Simplified

Definition: a hand

114

Beginnings—Worship of God

Analysis: We have observed God's hand(s) as ᗪ (爪, R. 87); and 𠂇, as in 甲 [申 , R. (144)]. These show God's hand(s) reaching down from above. But, man's hand(s) most often reach upward, often in worship, as in *hand(s)* ⼿ 61 ⼿ 62 (手, 扌). Note *to do obeisance, to pay one's respects to, to visit* 拜 63 (拜), where ⼿ is a worshipping *hand*, and ⽰ is the Godhead. Also examine *to praise* 昜, 揚 64 (揚) that shows the man with uplifted *hands* ⼿ , ⼿ in praise, and *God* 丅 (示 , R. 113) represented as a *King, Ruler* 王 (王), His glory is portrayed by the *sun* ⊙ (日 , R. 72).

Radical 55 (51)

Oracle bone Bronzeware Traditional Simplified

Definition: hands joined

Analysis: For the most part, rather than *joined hands* 𦥑 (廾) appearing in various characters, there are two hands 𦥑, probably of two persons, in worshiping mode. For example, *to give, confer* 畀 65 (畀) where the *hands* 𦥑 are worshipping in the *garden* 田 (田 , R. 102) on the mountain portrayed as ⌒. We do find the "hands joined" in *strange, unfamiliar* 異, 異 66 (異), showing the hands 𦥑 of the first couple worshiping outside the *garden* 田 in an unfamiliar place after they had been expelled from the garden.

To work together, all, the whole 共 67 (共) reveals the first couple with upraised *hands* 𦥑 worshiping a *Person* 口 (丁), Jesus Christ.

The Beginning of Chinese Characters

Radical 124 (183)

羽 羽

Oracle bone   Bronzeware   Traditional   Simplified

Definition: wings, feathers

Analysis: Does God have *wings, feathers* [68] (羽)? It would seem so from Psalm 91: 4:

> He shall cover you with
> <u>His feathers</u>,
> And under <u>His wings</u>
> you shall take refuge.

However, we must refer to other Bible texts as well, such as:

> Give ear, O Shepherd of Israel,
> You who lead Joseph
> like a flock;
> <u>You who dwell between the
> cherubim</u>, shine forth!
> (Psalm 80: 1)

We find that in the Hebrew sanctuary [see Appendix II] God's holy presence, the "Shekinah glory," dwelt between and under the outstretched wings of the golden cherubim [angels] that stood on the mercy seat in the cubical "Most Holy Place." God had communicated with Moses, the Hebrew leader, from this position.

> Now when Moses went into the tabernacle of meeting [sanctuary] to speak with Him [God], he heard the voice of One speaking to him from above the mercy seat that was on the ark of the Testimony, from <u>between the two cherubim</u>... (Numbers 7: 89)

So the *wings* (羽) belonged not to God, but to the "covering

Beginnings—Worship of God

angels." Note also the ◇ (、, R. 3) symbol indicating holiness. Thus when we examine the character *to learn, receive training, habit, custom* 習 69 (習), we may know that God was *speaking* ⊖ (曰, R. 73) from beneath the *wings* 羽 (羽) of the cherubim that overshadowed His throne. The *Shuo Wen* character 107 actually incorporates the Holy *Mountain* 山 (山, R. 46) in the radical for *speaking* , ⊟ (曰, R. 73), indicating therefore the site of His "training" session was from under the cherubim angels' wings, on the Holy Mountain.

Radical 176

  面

Oracle bone   Bronzeware   Traditional   Simplified

Definition: face, front, before, face-to-face, in person
Analysis: "Face-to-face" is "eye-to-eye," so once again, in this new pictogram, we are shown the place where the first couple encountered God. *Before, in person, face-to-face* 70 71 (面 , 面) tell us that this is on the Holy *Mount* ⌐ (厂, R. 27), in the presence of the *King* (首, R. 185) of the universe. The character 72 (古) at the top of the bronzeware means *ancient,* and portrays God's creative *mouth* ∀ . *Clay, earth* (土, R. 32), represents earth's first man Adam, who was created from the "dust of the ground." All of this tells us that God is the Creator from the beginning, from *ancient* days.

117

The Beginning of Chinese Characters

Radical 109 (145)

      Oracle bone Bronzeware Traditional Simplified

Definition: eye, look on, chief, most important

Analysis: The *eye* , 〖 73   〗 74 (目) in the Chinese calligraphy is *chief, most important!* We will see this to be true in 〖 (首, R. 185), with the eye's depiction of the source of the Fountain of Life on the Holy Mountain, and of God, Himself. The oracle bone symbol for *eye* 〖 has unmistakable resemblance to the *hill, cliff* 厂 (厂, R. 27), one symbol for the Holy Hill. How interesting also that the *eye* contains the *sun* ⊙ (日, R. 72), representing the glory of God.

The character *reach to, be with, together with* 〖 75   〗 76 (衆) implies that someone is traveling to be together with God. The site for the visit is apparent, for from the eye flows water—not tears, but *water* 〣 (水, R. 85) from the River of Life.

> . . . *You give them [the children of men] drink from*
> *the river of Your pleasures,*
> *For with You is the fountain of life;*
> *In your light we see light.*
>   (Psalm 36: 8-10).

Radical 181 (170)

      Oracle bone Bronzeware Traditional Simplified

Definition: leaf of a book, the head

Analysis: If God were writing a book of all humanity, Adam would be

Beginnings—Worship of God

the first *leaf of the book*, even *the head* 77 78 (頁) of the human race. This radical actually depicts the creation of Adam , (卩 , R. 26), the first man, from God, Himself, who is the *Chief, Head, Beginning* , (首 , R. 185).

God, whose dwelling place is in the very center of the Garden of Eden, on the Holy Mount, is the *beginning, the first, the head* 79 (首). Here, God Y arises from the *eye* ⊙ (目 , R. 109), in the center of the garden.

In Revelation 1: 8, we read:

"I am the Alpha and the Omega, the <u>Beginning</u> and the End," says the Lord, "who is and who was and who is to come, the Almighty,"

The "Almighty" One, the "Beginning" is the Creator, Jesus Christ.

Radical 131 (164)

Oracle bone   Bronzeware   Traditional   Simplified

Definition: a statesman, subjugate, conquer

Analysis: Another eye! This radical meaning a *statesman, to subjugate* 80 81 (臣) must ultimately refer to God's all-seeing eye. But look what it becomes when we turn it on its side —the Holy Mountain! The central peak is decorated with a black dot ● meaning "holy" [see (天), (R. 37)].

An interesting, rather formidable character, *to inspect* 82 (監) uses this "eye" as a head attached to a *Person* (人), and represents God. The object being inspected is a *vessel* (皿 , R. 108), composed of two back-to-back *persons* , the first couple.

The Beginning of Chinese Characters

Yet another character clearly reveals the all-seeing Godhead, *come near to, be with* 〖〗₈₃ (臨). This time the *person* 〖〗 (人) represents either Adam or the woman who is approaching the Godhead of three *Mouths, Persons* 〖〗 (口, R. 30), portrayed as 〖〗.

The phrase, "**Shangdi [God] be with you**"[84] (上帝臨汝) is used repeatedly in the *Shi Jing*.

Radical 184 (216)

Oracle bone Bronzeware Traditional Simplified

Definition: food, to eat, drink, to feed

Analysis: The radical 〖〗, 〖〗 [85] (食) meaning *food, to eat, drink* shows a *mouth* 〖〗 (口) turned upside down 〖〗, 〖〗 **(see** 〖〗, under R. 26), indicating God's mouth. The words of God's *mouth* were to be spiritual *food* for Adam, the man of dust 〖〗 and his wife (portrayed as a *sun*-like 〖〗 person).

In *to eat, food* 〖〗 [86] (飡) we can clearly see God, the *Person* 〖〗 (人) who is the source of Adam and Eve's spiritual food 〖〗 (食).

Jesus said:

> "*Man shall not live by bread alone,*
> *but by <u>every word that proceeds from</u>*
> *<u>the mouth of God</u>.*" *(Matthew 4. 4)*.

Radical 186 (214)

Oracle bone Bronzeware Traditional Simplified 香 香

Beginnings—Worship of God

Definition: fragrant, delicious, beautiful, tasty, incense

Analysis: The first couple surely found fruit from the tree 朩 (木, R. 75) of life, *fragrant, delicious, beautiful* 鬯 87 (香). Not only the fruit, but the *water* 巛 (水, R. 85) from the river of life was also *delicious* 鬯 88 (香), according to the *Shuo Wen* # 256 pictogram that shows not only the tree 朩, but even the *Holy Mountain* 冂 with the river of life 巛 flowing from it. Note also the *mouth* ㄩ, indicating that words from God's *mouth* ㄩ were indeed delicious and beautiful.

> How sweet are Your words to
> my taste,
> Sweeter than honey to my
> mouth!
> (Psalm 119: 103).

Radical 99 (135)

 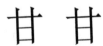

Oracle bone Bronzeware Traditional Simplified

Definition: sweet, pleasant, enjoy, voluntarily

Analysis: When Adam and his wife visited with God on the Holy Mount, they had voluntarily made the climb in order to enjoy the *sweet* ㄩ 89 (甘) fellowship and communion there. This radical ㄩ is pictographic, and cleverly conveys several ideas. The mouth ㄩ (口), being versatile, can do this! First, it conveys the idea of talking together (with God) in enjoyable conversation. But the mouth can also enjoy the sweet, pleasant ㄩ (甘) fruit from the tree of life and water from the river of life 鬯 (香, under the previous R. 186).

There was perfect *harmony* and *loyalty* 厰 90 (厭) at this time between the couple and God. This character portrays the hill 厂 (厂, R. 27),

121

with its two *trees* 㧴 (木, R. 75), thus depicting the site at the very center of the Garden of Eden, near the throne of God [see 㫃 (都 , under R. 163)]. The scene is *pleasant* 曰 (甘) as they converse and eat fruit from the tree of life. Unfortunately, this *harmony and loyalty* 㗊 would not always exist, as we shall soon learn.

Radical 53 (44)

Oracle bone Bronzeware Traditional Simplified

Definition: a covering, roof, (hill, mountain)

Analysis: Although today this radical usually refers to the roof of a building, originally, it was doubtless meant to represent a mountain or hill, specifically. The Holy Hill of the Garden of Eden, of course, was the home of the first couple. The original radicals ⌒ 91 ⌒ 92 (广) do resemble a house, yet there is similarity also to other radicals indicating a hill or mountain, e.g.: 厂 (厂 , R. 27); ⼳ (方 , R. 70); 囮 (面 , R. 176).

We have learned that the original sanctuary or temple was the Holy Mountain where the first couple met face-to-face with God. The character *temple* 㢅 93 (廟) in the bronzeware shows two members of the Godhead as 屮 (see 甶 , under R. 101); the *sun* ⊙ (日 , R. 72) symbolizes the third member of the Godhead. The *River* 川 (川 , R. 47) of Life pinpoints the site on the mountain. The character 㫰 94 (朝) by itself means *morning, morning worship*. So it becomes evident that Adam and his wife went to the Holy Mountain temple 㢅 each *morning* 㫰 to *worship* God.

An *imperial court* 㢋 95 (庭) must have originally been "open" on the sacred mountain when communion was held with God. The listening and speaking are evident from the *ear* 耳 (耳 R. 128) and *mouths* 吅 . The two characters 朝庭 used together mean "an imperial court where the king's office is located."

Radical 128 (163)

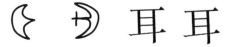

Oracle bone Bronzeware Traditional Simplified

Definition: ear, projection

Analysis: Yes, the clever Chinese have another "Holy Mountain" body part—this time the *ear* ᛝ ⁹⁶ ᚦ ⁹⁷ (耳). If these symbols are turned as ᗰ , ᗰ , their intent becomes obvious. There on that sacred mount, was a "listening" place for Adam and his wife.

The character *to listen, obey, understand* ⁹⁸ (聽) has not only the *ear* ᛝ , but also two *mouths* ᛒ for communication. In the character *to hear, learn, make known* ⁹⁹ (聞). The man also has both an *ear* ᛝ and a *mouth* ᗡ .

Beautifully constructed, the character *holy* ¹⁰⁰ (聖) has a *person* ᐱ with *ear* ᛝ and *mouth* ᗡ properly atuned. In the character *sound, voice* ¹⁰¹ (聲), we find that Adam had fellowship with God and could come to meet God Ψ on the holy *hill* ⌐ (⌐, R. 27) and hear His *voice* (with the *ear* ᛕ (耳).

Radical 89

×
× 　　　　　交

Oracle bone Bronzeware Traditional Simplified

Definition: to change, intertwine, communicate

Analysis: This radical *to change, intertwine* × ¹⁰² (爻) commonly reflects the changing which takes place in the mind with intertwining ideas. This is best illustrated by two characters. *To teach, educate, a religion* 教 103 教 104 (教) show the *Father* (父, R. 88) *intertwining* ✕ His thoughts with the thoughts of His *offspring, son* (Adam) (子, R. 39). In 教 the *intertwining* ✕ symbol takes the form of a mountain ∧ , suggesting the site of the teaching session.

The second similar character, *to study, learn, train up* 學 105 (歷) reveals God's *hands* (臼, R. 134) *training up, changing* ✕ the thoughts of the *son, offspring* on the mountain ∩ (∩, R. 14). This character with God's hands *"training up"* 學 is reminiscent of *to instruct* 申 (申, under R. 113), where God is holding the first *perfect* | (十, R. 24) man in His *hands* , instructing him. At any rate, the first educational process certainly took place in Eden with the Father-God as the Teacher, and the first couple as students.

Radical 105(154)

癶 兆

Oracle bone Bronzeware Traditional Simplified

Definition: back to back

Analysis: This radical has no free-standing oracle bone or bronzeware forms, but makes use of the symbols *to arrive at, stop, rest* 106 (止, R. 77). The *Shuo Wen* radical 274 (兆) has the appearance of two persons resting on a mount. This configuration is probably derived from the following character: *to ascend, rise, to take* 107 108 (登) where mounting feet, as , are *taking* an offering in their *hands* that are upraised in worship.

In turn, the *Father* (父, R. 88) *issues, reveals, discloses* 109 (發) His word to the first couple as they come before Him.

Beginnings—Worship of God

Radical 185

Oracle bone Bronzeware Traditional Simplified

Definition: the beginning, head, chief, first, king, God

Analysis: This is a radical of considerable significance. The peculiar shape of the oracle bone symbols meaning *beginning, head, leader, first, king* ⌇, ⌇ 110 (首), in the bronzeware, take on the interpretation of an eye with meaningful appendages ⌇ , ⌇ 011 (首). There are a number of features of ⌇ to point out. First, note the 111 , indicating the "presence of God (彡 , R. 59). Then, the large black dot • is a characteristic of holiness, as we find it in 大 (天 , R. [90]). So we immediately expect this is a place related to God. We previously met one other irregularly-shaped radical in the oracle bone—*abyss, deep* ⌇ (淵 , see under R. 85, 144 and 106). Because of the *river* ⌇ (川, R. 47) contained in it, we interpreted this as the Source of the River of Life and the *fountain* ⌇ (泉 , under R. 106) of Life. God, Himself is that *Fountain*—which brings us full circle—almost!

Now let us examine carefully the bronzeware figures ⌇ , and ⌇ . Obviously ⌇ has become an *eye* ⌇ (see also 目, R. 109). The "presence of God" 111 (彡 , R. 59) is again found. In ⌇ , we even find "God" ⊦ (卜 , R. 25) designated. The figure ⌇ portrays the Holy *Mountain* ⌇ with an eye in the center. There is no argument that God is represented by the definition of this radical: *the Beginning, Head, Chief, Leader, King, First.*

| Mountain | + | eye | + | rainbow of God's Presence | = | the Beginning First, Head |

125

Now, let us define the *Dao, the Way* 道 [112] (道). Literally, this may be interpreted as *walking* ⼻ ⼁ (辶, R. 144) to *the Head, God* 首. This would indicate that the original worship, an eye-to-eye meeting of man (Adam and the woman) with God, took place on the Holy Mountain of Eden. Recall that the *Dao* represented the Godhead (see under R. 1, p. ; also next R. 162).

Radical 162 (47)

Oracle bone   Bronzeware   Traditional   Simplified

Definition: walking

Analysis: In this beautiful radical, *walking* 辶 [113] (辶), the Chinese have forever immortalized the goal of walking—to the *"crossroad"* ⼻⼁ (行, R. 144, fully explained in Section VI, p. 200), on the Holy Mountain where they could *stop, rest* ⺗ (止, R. 77). This was the *way, road, path* 道 (道, see important discussion under previous R. 185) to meet with God, portrayed by the radical meaning *the Beginning, Head, King, First* 首 (首, R. 185). Since this character 道 (道) has come to indicate *Dao* [Tao], the Way, the Truth, and a mystical doctrine, it would be well at this point to clarify its meaning according to the ancient Chinese classical writing, as well as this foregoing character-analysis.

From earliest time, the ancient Chinese sage-kings taught the *Dao*, **the Way** 道 (道)[114] as the basis of their religious thinking and belief. But what is the Dao? According to the sage, Lao Zi (c. 570 **B.C.**), writing in his *Dao De Jing,* he defined the Dao thus:

> The Dao exists as one.
> One exists as two
> Two exists as three.
> And three create everything.[115]

Beginnings—Worship of God

This ancient mystery may now be solved! From our study of the divine Creator-Godhead (Section I), we learned that the Hebrew and Chinese Deity consists of three Persons: God the Father, God the Son [Jesus Christ], and God the Holy Spirit. They are three separate Persons, but their purpose is one. The Dao therefore may represent all three Members of the Godhead, or any One, such as Jesus Christ who Himself declared, "*I am <u>the way, the truth,</u> and <u>the life</u>. No one comes to the Father except through Me.*" (John 14: 6). A second character meaning *to lead, guide, instruct* 导 [116] (導) shows a worshiping *hand* indicating the ancient worship of the Dao. Considerably more will be learned regarding the Holy Mountain and its significance in Section VI.

Section III of this study of the ancient Chinese radicals has shown an amazing number of these primitive elements of their writing dedicated to memorializing the first couple's worship on the Holy Mountain of Eden. Most interesting has been the use of the eye, ear, and mouth—normally used in communication with God—to pictographically represent the Holy Mountain itself! Surely the ancient Chinese did not want this sacred place where man and God met, to be forgotten. Adam and his wife had much to learn from their divine Teacher who desired only their highest good.

A clarification of the Dao [Tao], not as a mystical, unsolvable puzzle, but as the true Godhead of Three, faithfully worshiped and obeyed by the early Chinese rulers—is indeed important!

God's one explicit command, that the first couple should ***not*** eat of the Tree of the Knowledge of Good and Evil, must be kept in mind. God had also warned them of an enemy to be avoided. In the next Section, we will learn of the cunning of the enemy, and of their sad fall into disobedience!

[1] Chung-kuo k'e-hsueh-yuan k'ao-ku yen-chiu-so, *Kchia-Ku Wen-Pien* (Peking: K'ao-ku-hsueh chuan-k'an yi-chung ti-shih-ssu hao, 1965), No. 13.9. [Hereafter abbreviated CKWP].
[2] Ma Wei Ching, *Wei Ching Chia Ku Wen Yuan* (Yunlin: Ma Fu Distributor, 1971), p. 107. [Hereafter abbreviated MWC].
[3] Ibid., p. 589.
[4] Ibid., p. 105.
[5] Hung Pei Chiang, *Ching Wen P'ien Ching Wen* (Taipei: Kung I Publ. Co., 1974), no. 9.11. [Hereafter abbreviated HPC].
[6] MWC, p. 413.
[7] HPC, no. 9,11.
[8] Ibid.
[9] HPC, no. 9.11.
[10] MWC, p. 105.
[11] CKWP, no, 13.10.
[12] MWC, p. 462.
[13] HPC, no. 13.6.
[14] MWC, p. 461.
[15] Ibid., p. 463.
[16] Wu Shuping and Lai Changyang, *The Four Books and Five Jing in Modern Chinese*, (Beijing: International Culture Publishing Co., Inc., 1996), Vol. III, *Shi Jing*, p. 331.
[17] MWC, p. 81.
[18] HPC, no. 9.13.
[19] CKWP, no. 10.8.
[20] Ibid., no. 9.7.
[21] Jia Gu Wen, *Zi Shuo Li* (Taiwan: An Guo Jun, 1983), p. 97. [Hereafter abbreviated ZSL].
[22] HPC, no. 7.14.
[23] Ibid., no. 1.2.
[24] Ibid.., no. 1.5.
[25] CKWP, no. 9.7.
[26] HPC, no. 9.16.
[27] Ibid., no. 11.6.
[28] Ibid., no. 11.6.
[29] CKWP, No. 14.4.

30. Ibid., no. 14.4.
31. Ibid., no. 14.5.
32. ZSL, p. 18.
33. HPC, no. 14.14.
34. CKWP, no. 14.4.
35. Ibid., no. 14.4.
36. HPC, no. 10.15.
37. Ibid., no. 4.17.
38. Ibid., no. 4.16.
39. Ibid., no. 10.15.
40. CKWP, no. 14.18.
41. HPC, no. 14.34.
42. MWC, p. 1379..
43. CKWP, no. 3.9.
44. HPC, no. 3.15.
45. CKWP, no. 7.13.
46. HPC, no. 7.18.
47. MWC, p. 160.
48. HPC, no. 7.21.
49. CKWP, no. 2.31.
50. MWC, p. 750.
51. HPC, no. 2.32.
52. Ibid., no. 14.14.
53. MWC, p. 664.
54. HPC, no. 14.14.
55. MWC, p. 664.
56. Lin Chih Ch'ing, *Ting Cheng Liu Shu T'ung* (Shanghai: Kuang-I Publ. Co., 1936) Section VII, p. 29. [Hereafter abbreviated LCC].
57. CKWP, no. 8.15.
58. MWC, p. 708.
59. Ibid., p. 708.
60. Ibid.
61. MWC, p. 557.
62. HPC, no. 12.6.
63. HPC, no. 12.6.

64 Ibid., no. 12.7 and 12.8.
65 MWC, p. 608.
66 HPC, no. 3.14.
67 CKWP, no. 3.7.
68 CKWP, no. 4.5.
69 Ibid., no., 4.5.
70 MWC, p. 704.
71 Ibid., p. 705.
72 Ibid., no. 3.2.
73 CKWP, no. 4.1.
74 HPC, no. 4.1.
75 CKWP, No. 4.1.
76 HPC, no. 4.1.
77 CKWP, no. 9.1.
78 HPC, no. 9.1.
79 MWC, p. 774.
80 CKWP, no. 3.20.
81 HPC, no. 3.30.
82 Ibid., no. 8.12.
83 Ibid., no. 8.12.
84 Wu Shupeng, op. cit., *Shu Jing*, p. 262.
85 MWC, p. 1108.
86 CKWP, no. 8.4.
87 MWC, p. 173.
88 Ibid., p. 174
89 Ibid., p. 728.
90 Bernhard Karlgren, *Grammata Serica* (Taipei: Ch'eng-wen Publ. Co., 1966) p. 279.
91 MWC,np. 1217.
92 HPC, no. 9.15.
93 Ibid., no. 9.15.
94 HPC, no. 7.3.
95 MWC, p. 1189.
96 CKWP, no. 12.3.
97 HPC, no. 12.5.
98 ZSL, p. 156.
99 CKWP, no. 12.3.
100 Ibid., no. 12.3.
101 Ibid. no. 12.3.
102 CKWP, no. 3.33.
103 Ibid., no. 3.28
104 MWC, p. 1331.
105 HPC, no. 3.38
106 Ibid., no. 2.18.

[107] CKWP, no. 2.16.
[108] HPC, no. 2.18.
[109] MWC, p. 676.
[110] CKWP, no. 9.1.
[111] HPC, no. 9.2.
[112] Ibid., no. 2.25.
[113] CKWP, no. 2.19.
[114] Samuel Wang and Ethel R. Nelson, *God and the Ancient Chinese* (Dunlap, TN: Read Books Publisher, 1998), pp. 14, 61-71.
[115] Gia Fu Feng and Jane English, *Translation of Lao Zi, Tao Te Ching* (Toronto: Vintage Books, Random House, Inc., 1989), Ch. 42, p. 44.
[116] HPC, no. 2.25.

The Beginning of Chinese Characters

Section IV

BEGINNINGS—SIN

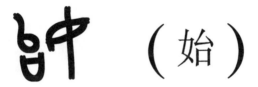

He [the devil] was a murderer from the beginning, and does not stand in the truth, because there is no truth in him. . . for he is a liar and the father of it.
(John 8: 44)

Beginnings—Sin

The previous sections have shown God's creation of the earth and its contents in six days. We also learned that the pinnacle of His creative work was His creation of the first two humans, Adam and his wife.

Originally, the first couple enjoyed a close, loving relationship with Shangdi, their Creator-God. Sad events took place, however, that destroyed this relationship and separated them from their kind and beneficent Creator.

There had been just one restriction which God placed upon the man and woman in the garden.

Genesis 2:16, 17

> And the LORD God commanded the man, saying, "Of every tree of the garden you may freely eat; "but of the tree of the knowledge of good and evil you shall not eat, for in the day that you eat of it you shall surely die."

Both Adam and his wife clearly understood God's command. Actually, God was giving them a test of loyalty. One day, the woman wandered away from the side of her husband. Curiosity led her to the forbidden tree where she encountered a strange, beautiful creature—a talking serpent.

Genesis 3: 1-6

> Now the serpent was more cunning than any beast of the field which

the LORD God had made. And he said to the woman, "Has God indeed said, 'You shall not eat of every tree of the garden'?"

And the woman said to the serpent, "We may eat the fruit of the trees of the garden: but of the fruit of the tree which is in the midst of the garden, God has said, 'You shall not eat it, nor shall you touch it, lest you die.'"

And the serpent said to the woman, "You will not surely die."

"For God knows that in the day you eat of it your eyes will be opened, and you will be like God, knowing good and evil."

So when the woman saw that the tree was good for food, that it was pleasant to the eyes, and a tree desirable to make one wise, she took of its fruit and ate. She also gave to her husband with her, and he ate.

Radical 75 (94)

Oracle bone   Bronzeware   Traditional   Simplified

Definition: tree, wooden, timber

Analysis: The *tree(s)* 朩 [1] (木) are a central focus in this study, and have already been met on a number of occasions. The original mandate of God to man concerned the tree of the knowledge of good and evil. If they ate from this forbidden tree, the penalty would be death.

Is there a pictograph portraying the tree of life from which the first couple could freely eat? It would seem that the character meaning *rich and full, awe-inspiring* [2] (栗), fits this magnificent, *fiery* ∀ (火, R. 86) tree. These three *fires* represent the fiery glory of the Godhead, for the Hebrew Scriptures say:

> *For the LORD God is a sun and shield;*
> *The LORD will give grace and glory;*
> *No good thing will He withhold*
> *From those who walk uprightly. (Psalm 84: 11).*

Beginnings—Sin

God provided a *rich and full* 㮚 (栗) life as the first couple ate from this tree. Might there also be a graph representing the tree of the knowledge of good and evil? The character *to die, perish* 喪 ³ (喪) shows two *mouths* 吅 (口 , R. 30) and two *hands* indicating that if the two persons, Adam and his wife, reached out with their hands to pluck the fruit, and ate from this tree 喪 , the result would be *death*.

From the graph *restrict, prevent* 杜 ⁴ (杜), it is clearly evident that God had placed a *restriction* on Adam, the man of *dust* 土 (土 , R. 32). God had designed that they should live forever, eating from the tree of life. But they were not to eat from this second tree. If they disobeyed God in this simple command, death would result.

Radical 175 (205)

非 非 非 非
Oracle bone Bronzeware Traditional Simplified

Definition: wrong, bad, negative, not
Analysis: The command *not* 非 ⁵ (非) to eat fruit from the tree of the knowledge of good and evil was given first to Adam, but included his wife, who was created later. To act contrary to God's command was *bad, wrong* 非 (非). Therefore, the two *persons* (人 , R. 9) were commanded *not* 非 (非) to pick fruit with their *hands* from the forbidden tree.

Interestingly, the bronzeware graph for this radical, *not, wrong, bad* 非 ⁶ (非) pictures the backs of God's hands turned to each other, thereby making a negative expression.

Radical 129

Oracle bone Bronzeware Traditional Simplified

The Beginning of Chinese Characters

Definition: a command, teaching, a pencil, suddenly

Analysis: Here is another graph that refers to God's *command* 󰀀 7 (聿) to Adam (and his wife) not to use a *hand* 󰀀 (手) to pick fruit from the forbidden *tree* 󰀀 (木 , R. 75). In this pictograph only the roots of the forbidden tree are drawn 󰀀.

In the character *law* 󰀀 8 (律), Adam was not to take a *long walk* 󰀀 (彳, R. 54) to the forbidden *tree* 󰀀 and use his *hand* 󰀀 to pick fruit from it. This was God's *Law* 󰀀 (律).

tree   hand   command   long walk   law

Radical 154

󰀀   󰀀   貝   贝

Oracle bone   Bronzeware   Traditional   Simplified

Definition: precious, valuable, cowrie

Analysis: In God's sight, Adam and Eve were very *precious, valuable* 󰀀 󰀀 9 󰀀 10 (貝). In 󰀀 we find God's creative hands. However, in 󰀀 we see two conjoined *persons* 󰀀 and *fire* 󰀀 (火 , R. 86), indicating their glorious, fiery appearance, for they had been created in God's image. However, in the bronzeware 󰀀 , God's arms and hands are depicted as 󰀀 and the first couple by 󰀀 and by *two* 二 (二, R. 7). (See also Radicals 193, 206, and 132).

In the character, *responsibility, to obey* 󰀀 11 (責), we find *Di [Shangdi, God]* 󰀀 (see discussion under R. 30, p. 21). The *precious* 󰀀 couple were *responsible to obey* God. In 󰀀 , the Holy Spirit 󰀀 (矢, R. 111), with the other two members of the Godhead represented by two God radicals ┝ + ┑ (see R. 113), form *Shangdi* 帝 (上帝). Obedience to God was of vital importance.

> *Fear God and keep His*
> *commandments,*
> *For this is the whole duty of*
> *man. (Ecclesiastes 12: 13).*

Radical 132 (180)

  自 自

Oracle bone   Bronzeware   Traditional   Simplified

Definition: origin, source, invite, the nose, self

Analysis: Once again, *origin, source, self* ¹² (自) clearly portrays the Holy Mountain as △ (山 , R. 46). The Chinese concept of origins at this site is found by symbolizing the first couple as *two* = persons. Compare *precious* 貝 (貝 , R. 154). They were, of course, the ultimate *origin, source* of the human family.

At this site on the Holy Mountain, the original *law, rule* 泉 ¹³ (泉) was given by God:

> *And the LORD God commanded the man, saying, "Of every tree of the garden you may freely eat; but of the tree of the knowledge of good and evil you shall not eat, for in the day that you eat of it you shall surely die." (Genesis 2: 16, 17).*

This was a *law, rule* given the first couple to exercise their loyalty and obedience to their benefactor and Creator-God. In 泉 is the forbidden *tree* 木 (木 , R. 75). Furthermore, in the character *to cut off [the nose], to destroy, maim* 劓 ¹⁴ (劓) we find the dire result of disobedience and willful eating of the forbidden *tree* 木. The *knife* 刂 (刂 , R. 18) symbol-

139

izes death as the result of eating the forbidden fruit and the future sacrifices of innocent animals necessary to atone for this disobedience and sin (see *beginning* [of sin] under R. 145, p. 168).

Radical 165 (197)

Oracle bone   Bronzeware   Traditional   Simplified

Definition: to separate, distinguish

Analysis: Adam and his wife were to *distinguish* 15 (釆) between the two trees in the midst of the garden. Eating fruit from the tree of life would give them immortality, whereas eating fruit from the tree of the knowledge of good and evil would result in death.

This character is sometimes confused with a similar one meaning *to pluck, gather* 16 (采) in which the *tree* is planted by God's *hand* (爪 , R. 87), and according to the oracle bone graph 17 (果), this represents the forbidden tree . The meaning of , *consequence, certainty, surely*—sounds ominous! Especially so when the *woman* (女) is found kneeling before the tree, coveting the *beautiful* 18 (媄) fruit!

Radical 153 (198)

Oracle bone   Bronzeware   Traditional   Simplified

Definition: a fabulous beast, reptile without feet, to pose as moral peer, to discriminate.

Beginnings—Sin

Analysis: The radical, *a fabulous beast, pose as a moral peer* 豸 [19] (豸) surely is a good description of the devil. The oracle bone writing shows a *mouth* ᗡ (口) on its side and a *person* 𠂉 (人). This *fabulous beast* 豸 spoke to Eve with his *mouth* � in a human voice, like a *person* 𠂉 , posing as a *moral peer,* by pretending he was morally superior to God. But who was this imposter? According to Genesis 3:1, he was a serpent *"more cunning than any beast of the field which the LORD God had made."*

The Hebrew Scriptures record how a mighty angel called Lucifer had rebelled against God's fair government of love in heaven. It was Lucifer's studied intent to destroy the loving relationship between God and the first couple. Scenes of what had taken place while Lucifer was in heaven are recorded in Ezekiel 28: 12, 13, 14-17:

> *Thus says the LORD God:*
> *"You were the seal of*
> *perfection,*
> *Full of wisdom and perfect in*
> *beauty.*
> *<u>You were in Eden, the garden</u>*
> *<u>of God;</u>...*
> *You were the anointed cherub*
> *who covers;*
> *I established you;*
> *<u>You were on the holy</u>*
> *<u>mountain of God;</u>...*
> *You were perfect in your ways*
> *from the day you were*
> *created,*
> *Till iniquity was found in you...*
>
> *You became filled with*
> *violence within,*
> *And you sinned*

> *Therefore I cast you as a*
> *profane thing*
> *Out of the mountain of God; . . .*
>
> *Your heart was lifted up*
> *because of your beauty;*
> *You corrupted your wisdom*
> *for the sake of your splendor;*
> *I cast you to the ground, . . ."*

First we should note here that in heaven there is also a "Garden of Eden" where God has His "Holy Mountain." It would seem, therefore, that the earthly Eden with its Holy Hill was a miniature of the great original in heaven! (See Section VI). It was from this sacred place that Lucifer was cast out to the earth. We learn more of Lucifer, the morning star, from Isaiah 14: 12-14:

> *"How you are fallen from*
> *heaven,*
> *O Lucifer, son of the morning!*
> *How you are cut down to the*
> *ground,*
> *You who weakened the*
> *nations!*
> *For you have said in your*
> *heart:*
> *'I will ascend into heaven,*
> *I will exalt my throne above*
> *the stars of God;*
> *<u>I will also sit on the mount of</u>*
> *<u>the congregation</u>*
> *On the farthest sides of the*
> *north;*
> *I will ascend above the heights*
> *of the clouds,*
> *I will be like the Most High.'"*

Beginnings—Sin

Lucifer was not satisfied with his high position among the angels. He wanted to usurp God's throne and sit on the Holy Mount. So he was cast out of heaven to earth with one third of the angels who joined him in his rebellion, as described in Revelation 12: 7-9:

> *And war broke out in heaven: Michael and his angels fought against the dragon; and the dragon and his angels fought, but they did not prevail, nor was a place found for them in heaven any longer. So the great dragon was cast out, that serpent of old, called the Devil and Satan, who deceives the whole world; he was cast to the earth, and his angels were cast out with him.*

Now, perhaps, we can begin to understand why Satan [Lucifer, the devil, that serpent of old] was intent on beguiling Adam and his wife and taking over the earthly Eden and its Holy Mountain! Let us now follow the sad events recorded in both the Hebrew Scriptures and the ancient Chinese characters. These describe the account of the first couple's temptation by the devil and their fall into sin.

Radical 44 (67)

Oracle bone   Bronzeware   Traditional   Simplified

Definition: corpse, representative of the dead

Analysis: The radical ⟨ [20] (尸), *corpse, representative of the dead*, is an apt description of the snake-like *person* ⟨ (人), the devil. Satan, in his rebellion, had cut himself off from God, the source of all life. He was spiritually dead, and eventually would become the instigator and representative of all those who rebel against God and are under the sentence of death.

The Beginning of Chinese Characters

The talking serpent was a *foreigner* 𡗞 ²¹ (夷) whose intent was to *kill*, *exterminate* 𡗞 (夷) the *noble* 大 (大) person (man or woman). Note the serpent-like individual 𠂆 (尸) who looms as a threat to the *noble* 大 person. The Garden of Eden had been given to the first couple by God, so the devil is rightly designated as a *foreigner* 𡗞 to Eden.

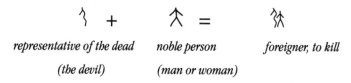

| representative of the dead | noble person | foreigner, to kill |
| (the devil) | (man or woman) | |

Radical 57 (71)

Oracle bone   Bronzeware   Traditional   Simplified

Definition: bow, curved

Analysis: The radical, *bow, curved* 𓏲 𠂆 ²² (弓) is identical to R. 44, *corpse, representative of the dead* 𠂆 (尸). This symbol 𓏲 again aptly describes the devil (Satan) in terms of a snake-like person whose plan is to kill (which is also the aim of using a *bow* 𓏲 with arrows or darts). How interesting that the Hebrew record encourages us all to put on special armor to protect from the darts (shot from the bow) of the devil. These darts are symbolic of his lies.

> *Above all, taking the shield of faith with which you will be able to quench all the fiery darts of the wicked one. (Ephesians 6: 16).*

When describing someone extremely suspicous, the Chinese have an interesting saying: (杯弓蛇影) **mistake the reflection of a *bow* in a cup for a *snake*** Therefore, *bow* and *snake* are clearly related in Chinese thought.

Beginnings—Sin

The woman had approached the forbidden tree alone, and there the talking serpent addressed her with the question, *"Has God indeed said, 'You shall not eat of every tree of the garden?'"* To which the woman replied: *"We may eat the fruit of the trees of the garden; but of the fruit of the tree which is in the midst of the garden, God has said, 'You shall not eat it, nor shall you touch it, lest you die.'" (Genesis 3: 1-3).*

The devil scoffingly answered, *"You will not surely die." (Genesis 3:4).* By this statement, the devil was completely *negating* 林 23 (弗) what God had said. Note that 林 (弗), *no, negative, not,* depicts the serpent resting in the two *trees* 林 that stood next to one another in the middle of the garden of Eden. A more common rendition of this character 弗 24 (弗), *no, negative, not,* portrays Adam and his wife, the two *perfect* | + | (十, R. 24) persons with the serpent ᠌ ensnaring them.

The woman was no match for the wily serpent. He was *strong, violent, compelling* 25 (弱) with his lying persuasion. In this graph, the snake-like person is molding her, the *person* into a someone just like himself as a result of his *compelling* words.

Radical 49 (72)

᠌   己   己

Oracle bone   Bronzeware   Traditional   Simplified

Definition: self, private, personal

Analysis: The radical, *self, personal private* ᠌ 26 (己) is another Chinese character describing the devil as a serpent who is only interested in *self,* and his own *personal* interests. Again, we find a snake-like figure ᠌ .

The character *jealous* 27 (忌), portrays the *selfish* ᠌ serpent,

The Beginning of Chinese Characters

the devil, whose *heart* 忄 was *jealous* of God, a rebellious attitude. The character 忌 also means *superstitious, avoid, shun*. Unfortunately, the woman failed to be cautious and *avoid, shun* 忌 the wicked serpent!

Radical 80

　　　　　　　　Oracle bone　Bronzeware　Traditional　Simplified

Definition: not, do not, negative, stop, forbid

Analysis: God's command to Adam *not* 毋 [28] (毋) to eat from the tree of the knowledge of good and evil, applied also to his wife. She, the first *woman* (女, R. 38), was *not* (毋) to eat the forbidden fruit. God had *forbidden* (毋) her to do so. Is it a coincidence that *forbid* (毋) and *mother* (母) are identical in the ancient oracle bone and bronzeware writings? It was Adam's wife, the first *mother* (母) of all, together with Adam, who were *forbidden* (毋), to eat of the tree of the knowledge of good and evil—yet she was the first to disobey God's specific command. Under the devil's cunning argument, she came to believe that she would not die, and that God was withholding good from her and Adam.

The steps in the temptation and fall of the woman are recorded in both the Chinese characters and the Hebrew Scripture:

> So when the woman saw that the tree was good for food, that it was pleasant to the eyes, and a tree <u>desirable</u> to make one wise, . . . (Genesis 3: 6)

Yes, the fruit was *desirable, covetable* [29] (婪). In this character, the *woman* is facing one *tree* 木 , *coveting* the fruit, with her

Beginnings—Sin

back to the second *tree* 木 , the tree of life.
   ...*she took of its fruit and ate. She also gave to her husband with her, and he ate. (Genesis 3: 6)*.

Radical 28 (37)   ꓘ   ♂   厶   厶

Oracle bone   Bronzeware   Traditional   Simplified

Definition: private, secret, a certain person

Analysis: We met this radical (doubled) in 💍 (幺 , R. 52) where the conjoined *perfect* 十 (十 , R. 24) couple is portrayed. *Private secret, certain person* ꓘ , ♂ ³⁰ ♂ (厶) is not found standing alone. The radical is used in various characters where it may take on any of the above meanings. After the first couple's creation, God had made them *landlords* 田 ³¹ (畯) of Eden. The graph ♂ (厶) in 𢀖 must therefore have represented a *certain person*, the woman, who is joined with Adam, the *kneeling man* ⼎ (卩 , R. 26). God made them landlords of the beautiful *garden* 田 (田 , R. 102). They were *loyal, sincere* 💍 ³² 💍 ³³ (允) to each other. In the bronzeware figure 💍 , the *woman* 乛 (女 , R. 38) is identified, so in 💍 , *sincere, loyal*, the *person* 𠆢 must represent the man, Adam. At any rate, they could *confide in* 💍 (允) each other.

However, one day, we find that the woman *goes away, is apart* 厽 ³⁴ (去) from her husband. In this graph, Adam is represented by the *noble* 大 person, and his wife is ○ , the *person* who *goes away* 厽 (去). By her separation from her husband, she becomes an easy prey for the wicked *foreigner* 夷 (夷 , see under R. 44), the serpent-devil whose intent is to *exterminate* 夷 the first couple.

As the *woman* 厽 is tempted by her *desire* 婪 (婪 , see under R.

The Beginning of Chinese Characters

80) to eat fruit from the forbidden *tree* 朿 (木), she reaches out her *hand* ㇂ , and plucks a fruit. She has by this act disobeyed God's one command. This is the *beginning* 㚸 *35* (始) of sin on the beautiful earth, for "sin" means the breaking of God's command, *law* 祂 (律 , see under R. 129). In the character *beginning* 㚸 (始), we find the *woman* 㐄 *secretly, privately* ↺ (厶) *eating* ㅂ , represented by a mouth. This unfortunate act has been best illustrated by a Seal character for *beginning* 㦧 *36* (始), where *secretly, privately* ↺ (厶) drops like a fruit into the open *mouth* ㅂ (口) of the *woman* 㐄 (女)!

Radical (192)

朿 朿 束 束

Oracle bone Bronzeware Traditional Simplified

Definition: to control, restrain, bind

Analysis: This graph clearly records that God had asked Adam *to control, restrain* 朿 , 朿 *37* (束) himself, and not eat with his *mouth* ㅂ , ○ (口) from the *tree* 朿 (木 , R. 75) of the knowledge of good and evil. Eating of this tree would cause him to sin and bring him into bondage with God's enemy, Satan.

It was God's *law, regulation*  *38* (索) that the first couple *control* 朿 their appetite. In 丅 , God is portrayed 丅 , and the forbidden tree is designated as the one over which one must exercise *control* ⚹ [朿]. However, when Adam learned that his beloved wife had been deceived by the serpent into eating the forbidden fruit, what was he to do? Why had she left his side, and out of curiosity, investigated the tree of the knowledge of good and evil? Would Adam lose his beautiful helpmate? It was a hard decision, but he *decided to go ahead without further consideration,* that he *might as well*

Beginnings—Sin

衤 39 (索) join Eve in her disastrous sin. He put out his *hand* 一 (扌) to pluck the fruit. No longer did he *refrain* 朿 (束) from eating ○ from the forbidden *tree* 朩 . It was a terrible, costly decision—not only for himself, but for his posterity as well!

Unfortunately, as we have seen, the first couple had failed the test of obedience, and *rebelled, acted contrary to* 衤 40 (逆) God's mandate and eaten the forbidden fruit. This character contains the graph *disobedient* 屰 41 (屰), which is simply a fallen man 大 (大). It was all because they had responded *fast, quickly* 辶 42 (速) to the invitation of the serpent, and had failed to *restrain* 朿 (束) themselves from eating fruit from the forbidden tree.

Radical 120 (77)

Oracle bone Bronzeware Traditional Simplified

Definition: silk, fine, delicate

Analysis: Although this radical does not appear by itself to be significant in the Genesis story, its character derivatives are! In *lineage, genealogy* 系 43 (系), the descendants 幺幺 of the first couple 𠂇 are found coming from God's *hand* 爪 (爪, R. 87)—which concept is in opposition to the evolutionary theory!

What was the *conclusion, end* 终 44 (終) of the first chapter in the life of Adam and Eve? Comparing 幺幺 with 幺幺 (above), it would seem that the first couple 幺幺 had fallen 幺幺! They must *die* 幺幺 (終), as a direct result of transgression of God's decree!

Thus it was that the first man and woman disobeyed God's one, simple command, given in love, not to eat of the tree of the knowledge of good and evil. Now they were facing the death sentence. The glorious covering light of God's likeness was fading, and they shamefully discovered they were naked. Instead of looking forward to God's frequent visit to the garden, they feared His approach.

Would God be as merciful as He had been loving? What did their future hold?

---

[1] Chung-kun k'e-hsueh-yuan K'an-ku yen-chiu-so, *Chia-Ku Wen-Pien* (Peking: K'ao-ku-hsueh chuan-k'an yi-chung ti-shih-ssu hao, 1965, no. 6.1. [Hereafter abbreviated CKWP].

[2] Ibid., no. 7.10.

[3] Ibid., no. 2.14.

[4] Ibid., no. 6.1.

[5] Jin Gu Wen, *Zi Shuo Li* (Taiwan: An Guo Jun, 1983), p. 153. (Hereafter abbreviated ZSI).

[6] Hung Pei Chiang, *Ching Wen P'ien Ching Wen* (Taipei: Kung I Publ. Co., 1974), No. 11.12. [Hereafter abbreviated HPC].

[7] CKWP, no. 3.19.

[8] Ibid., no. 2.25.

[9] Ibid., no. 6.10.

[10] HPC, no. 6.16.

[11] CKWP, no. 6.11.

[12] HPC, 4.5.

[13] CKWP, no. 6.2.

[14] HPC, no. 4.24.

[15] CKWP, no. 2.3.

[16] HPC, no. 6.5.

[17] CKWP, no. 6.2.

[18] Ma Wei Ching, *Wei Ching Chia Ku Wen Yuan* (Yunlin: Ma Fu Distributor, 1871), p. 134. [Hereafter abbreviated MWC].

19. CKWP, no. 9.11.
20. ZSI, p. 118.
21. Ibid., p. 139.
22. CKWP, no. 12.21.
23. MWC, p. 1357.
24. CKWP, no. 12.13.
25. Ibid., no. 12.21.
26. Ibid., no. 14.13.
27. HPC, no. 10.17).
28. ZSI, p. 164.
29. CKWP, no. 12.10.
30. HPC, no, 2.3; 4.16.
31. Ibid., no. 13.10.
32. Ibid., no. 8.24.
33. CKWP, no. 8.12.
34. HPC, no. 5.23.
35. Ibid., no. 12.17.
36. Lin Chih Ch'ing. *Ting Cheng Liu Shu T'ung* (Shanghai: Kuang-I Publ. Co., 1936), Section 2, part v, p. 2. [Hereafter abbreviated LCC].
37. CKWP., no. 6.9.
38. MWC, p. 1033.
39. Ibid.
40. CKWP, no. 2.19.
41. Ibid., no. 3.1.
42. MWC, p. 132.
43. CKWP, no. 12.22.
44. MWC, p. 1101.

The Beginning of Chinese Characters

Section V

BEGINNINGS—SALVATION

Knowing that you were not redeemed with corruptible things, . . . but with the precious blood of Christ, as of a lamb without blemish and without spot. He indeed was foreordained before the foundation of the world, but was manifest in these last times for you.
(1 Peter 1: 18-20)

Beginnings—Salvation

After Adam and his wife ate fruit from the forbidden tree, many changes immediately began to take place.

Genesis 3: 7-15:

> *Then the eyes of both of them were opened; and they knew that they were naked; and they sewed fig leaves together and made themselves coverings.*
> *And they heard the sound of the LORD God walking in the garden in the cool of the day, and Adam and his wife hid themselves from the presence of the LORD God among the trees of the garden.*
> *Then the LORD God called to Adam and said to him, "Where are you?"*
> *So he said, "I heard Your voice in the garden and I was afraid because I was naked; and I hid myself."*
> *And He said, "Who told you that you were naked? Have you eaten from the tree of which I commanded you that you should not eat?"*
> *Then the man said, "The woman whom You gave to be with me, she gave me of the tree, and I ate."*

And the LORD God said to the woman, "What is this you have done?" And the woman said, "The serpent deceived me, and I ate." So the LORD God said to the serpent:

> *"Because you have done this,*
> *You are cursed more than all cattle,*
> *And more than every beast of the field;*
> *On your belly you shall go,*
> *And you shall eat dust*
> *All the days of your life,*
> *And I will put enmity*
> *Between you and the woman,*
> *And between your seed and her Seed;*
> *He shall bruise your head,*
> *And you shall bruise His heel."*

What tragic scenes followed the first couple's disobedience! First, when they discovered that their glorious robes of innocence had faded and that they were naked, they were filled with horror since it was nearly time for God's daily visit. They quickly fashioned coverings of fig leaves. Then they tried to hide when they heard God approaching. But this was useless. When confronted with their disobedience, they began blaming not only each other, but the serpent tempter, and even God! At this point, the LORD cursed the serpent and proclaimed the first promise of a coming Savior who would one day destroy the enemy, but in so doing would Himself suffer greatly and die. We follow, now, the sequence of events as cataloged in the basic radicals. It is surprising how many Chinese radicals portray this evil serpent—enemy of man and God!

Radical 158 (200)

身　身　身

Oracle bone　Bronzeware　Traditional　Simplified

Definition: body, oneself, child in the womb

Analysis: The radical *body, oneself, child in the womb* 身 ¹ (身) is of considerable significance. Is it a coincidence that it is pronounced "Shen"—even as one of God's names is *Shen* 示乙 (神 , see under R. (144, p. 28), which pictures His Creatorship of the two original *Persons* 乚 (conjoined 人, R. 9). First, let us analyze *body, child in the womb* 身 (身). Here we find God as a *Person* 丁 creating a glorious, *sun*-like ⊙ (日 , see under R. 72) person (Adam) from the ground ＿ . So 身 (身) represents the creation of Adam from and by God.

Seal graphs of God, *Shen* 示, 示 ² show, in the first graph, conjoined "*suns*" 8 , representing both Adam and his wife. In 示 Adam is represented as arising from the ground ⊙ , while Eve has her origin in the man, Adam, in ⊚ . All this "detour" is to confirm that the *sun* ⊙ in 身 is Adam!.

After the first couple's disobedience, they must *hide, shun, avoid* 躲 ³ (躲) God. Note the *body* 身 (身), together with 朵 ⁴ (朵), meaning *a cluster of flowers or fruit*. A bending *person* 乚 (人) is seen within the *tree* 木 (木). All of this very aptly describes the couple's hiding in the flowering trees from God. Again from the Seal writing, we learn why they were hiding. They were *naked* 裸 ⁵ (裸). This time the *body* 身 is covered with *consequence, fruit of a tree* 果 ⁶ (果). Recall that the couple covered their nakedness with leaves from a fig tree, and also their nakedness was due to eating the forbidden *fruit* 果 (果) with dire *consequences*.

The Beginning of Chinese Characters

Radical 142 (174)

        Oracle bone Bronzeware Traditional Simplified

Definition: reptile, worm, insect

Analysis: This radical, *reptile, worm* 〇 , 〇 7 (虫) represents the devil who tempted Adam and his wife in the guise of a serpent (see Radicals 153, 44, 57 and 49). A part of the devil's punishment was to "go on his belly"—but far worse was to be his final extinction by the Savior who would "crush his head." Note again this prophecy:

> "And I will put enmity
> Between you and the   woman,
> And between your seed and
>   her Seed;
> He shall bruise your head,
> And you shall bruise His heel."
>   (Genesis 3: 15).

In the character *snake* 〇 8 (蛇), a *foot* 𠂆 is pictured about to step on and bruise or crush the head of the *serpent* 〇 (虫). However, in the process of defeating the devil, the *Seed, Offspring* 𠘧 (子, see R. 39) of the woman, the Son of God, would also suffer.

Radical 157 (196)

        Oracle bone Bronzeware Traditional Simplified

Definition: the foot, enough, full, complete, satisfied, excessive

Analysis: the oracle bone rendition of *foot, enough* 日 9 (足) is

158

Beginnings—Salvation

identical to the character *upright, virtuous, true, pure, original* 𠯖 (正 , see under R. 77), and therefore represents the foot of either Adam or his wife.

In *awe-struck* 𠣗 ¹⁰ (跽), a *snake* 𠃊 (己 R. 49) is seen above a *foot* 𠂆 (足 , R. 77). The first couple were *awe-struck* 𠣗 (跽) when they heard God's plan of salvation by which His Son, Jesus, the Seed of the woman, would crush the serpent's head. But in so doing, His heel (foot) would also be bruised— a prophesy that His feet would be nailed to the cross on which He died— not just for the first couple's sins— but for the sins of all humanity.

Radical 212

𠂉 𦫳 龍 龙

Oracle bone Bronzeware Traditional Simplified

Definition: the dragon

Analysis: From Revelation 12: 9, we read:

> "So the great <u>dragon</u> was cast out, that <u>serpent</u> of old, called the Devil and Satan, who deceives the whole world; he was cast to the earth, and his angels were cast out with him."

The Hebrew Scriptures use the term *dragon* 𢔇 , 𠂉 ¹¹ 𦫳 ¹² (龍) for the devil. The Chinese have a perfectly descriptive graph of the enemy Satan, especially in the bronzeware 𦫳 . In it we find a fallen person (Satan) from heaven 𠀁 (upright 立) targeting at the man and woman, represented by *flesh* 夕 (月 , R. 130). The devil becomes a *snake* 㔾 (甴 , R. 142) that speaks with his *mouth* 𠙵 (口) like a *person* 𠆢 (人). The oracle bone character 𠂉 (龍) tells the same story—a talking 𠙵 serpent 㔾 .

The character *reverential, to give, present to* 𦫳 ¹³ (巽) depicts the

159

The Beginning of Chinese Characters

dragon (龍) being worshiped by upraised *hands* (卄). The first couple had *given reverence to* (龑) the Devil-Serpent instead of God. They would now suffer the consequences.

Radical 103 (156)

Oracle bone   Bronzeware   Traditional   Simplified

Definition: the foot, a roll of cloth

Analysis: This radical *foot, roll of cloth* ¹⁴ (疋) is a simple picture of a foot—either Adam or his wife's foot, *stopping*. They had walked to the forbidden tree and presumptuously eaten its fruit. [It will be seen that *stop* (止, R. 77); *foot* (足, R. 157); *foot* (疋, R. 103) and *upright, true* (正 ; under R. 77) are used almost interchangeably].

What were some of the consequences of the man and woman's disobedience? We read again from Genesis 3: 16-19:

> To the woman He [God] said:
> "I will greatly multiply
> your <u>sorrow</u> and your conception;
> In pain you shall bring forth children;
> Your desire shall be for your husband.
> And he shall rule over you."
> Then to Adam He said, "Because you have heeded
> the voice of your wife, and have eaten from the tree
> of which I commanded you, saying, 'You shall not eat of it':
> "Cursed is the ground for your **sake**;
> In toil you shall eat of it
> All the days of your life.
> Both <u>thorns</u> and thistles

> *it shall bring forth for you,*
> *And you shall eat the herb*
> *of the field.*
> *In the sweat of your face*
> *you shall eat bread*
> *Till you return to the ground.*
> *For out of it you were taken;*
> *For dust you are,*
> *And to dust you shall return."*

From the above Scripture, it can be seen that *sorrow* and *thorns* 𣎴 [15] (楚) were two of the many consequences of their disobedience. This character shows a *person* 口 (丁) *stopping* 止 (止, R. 77) at the two *trees* 林 (林), the tree of life and the tree of the knowledge of good and evil. Their unfortunate stop and eating from the forbidden tree brought *sorrow, thorns* 𣎴 (楚) to them and all mankind.

The first two *persons* 亻 + 亻 (人) had made the fatal *stop* 止 (止) in the garden 甫 (甫, under R. 101). They had *stumbled, fallen* 蹇 [16] (蹇) into the devil's snare.

亻亻 + 甫 + 止 = 蹇

first couple   *garden*   *stop*   *stumble, fall*

Whereas the first name Adam had given his wife was "Woman," because she had been taken out of him, and they had become "one flesh," now he gave her a new name—apart from himself:

> *And Adam called his wife's name Eve,*
> *Because she was the mother of all living.*
>   *(Genesis 3: 20).*

Radical 78 (97)

歺   支 歹

Oracle bone   Bronzeware   Traditional   Simplified

Definition: vicious, bad, wicked (God on the Holy Mount)

Analysis: The definition *bad, wicked, vicious* 歺 17 (歹,支) does not refer to God on the Holy Mount, but to man whom God must condemn from His lofty seat of judgment. When sinful *man* 亻 (人) comes before God, it is because he is *obstinate, resolute, unchangeable* and therefore must be *condemned, to die* 歺亻 18 (死).

The character 凼 19 (葬) has been defined as *to bury, consign to the grave,* in keeping with the above definition of this radical. However, 洌 , 冽 20 (洌, 冽), *pure, clean, wash clean,* would seem to convey more of the original meaning of 歺. In these characters we find the river of life depicted as 巛 or ⋮ as it flows from the Holy Mount 冂. This would certainly suggest God's plan of cleansing from sin. Ultimately, the river of life is symbolic of Christ's shed blood on Mount Calvary, when He, as man's Creator-God would die a sacrificial death in mankind's stead, taking on Himself the sins of all who believe in Him. Jesus said,

> "For God so loved the world that He gave His only begotten Son [Jesus Christ], that whoever believes in Him should <u>not perish</u> but have everlasting life."   (John 3: 16).

Radical 178

草   韋   韋   韦

Oracle bone   Bronzeware   Traditional   Simplified

Definition: turn away from, against, go in opposite direction.

Analysis: The graph meaning *to turn away from* 㫃 [21] (韋) shows two feet 舛 walking in opposite directions on either side of 囗, a virtuous *Person*. The bronzeware 韋 [22] (韋) actually substitutes the graph 大 (方, see under R. 70), which we have interpreted as God.

After Adam and Eve rebelled against God, they did not want to meet Him, but went in an opposite direction and hid. The character *oppose, leave, deviate from, err, go against* 違 [23] (違) adds *walking* 彳 (辶, R. 162) to the feet going in opposite direction 舛.

At this point, it was necessary for God to give Adam and Eve the sad decree that they must leave their beautiful garden home:

Genesis 3: 22-24:

> Then the LORD God said, "Behold, the man has
> become like one of Us, to know good and evil.
> And now, lest he put out his hand and take also of
> the tree of life, and eat, and live forever" —
> therefore the LORD God sent him out of the garden
> of Eden to till the ground from which he was taken.
> So He drove out the man; and He placed cherubim
> at the east of the garden of Eden, and a flaming
> sword which turned every way to guard the way to
> the tree of life.

Thus we find that God must reluctantly expel the first couple from their lovely garden home. The gate of Eden became the barrier to keep them from eating from the tree of life and becoming immortal sinners.

Radical 166 (195)

Oracle bone Bronzeware Traditional Simplified

Definition: a lane, street, melancholy, sorrow

Analysis: the radical *melancholy, sorrow, lane, country* 畢 24 (里) shows Adam, the man of *dust* ⊥ (土, R. 32) outside the *garden* 田 (田, R. 102). He was full of *sorrow* 畢 as a result of being sent out of the garden.

The reason for the *dust* ⊥ man being exiled from the garden is apparent in the character meaning *wild, uncultivated, wilderness* 林⊥林 25 (埜). It was a direct result of his eating fruit from one of the two *trees* 林林 standing in the middle of the garden. Outside, the land was uncultivated.

Radical 194 (215)

畏　鬼　鬼　鬼

Oracle bone　Bronzeware　Traditional　Simplified

Definition: alien, spirit, devil, to return

Analysis: The radical 畏 26 鬼 27 (鬼) originally carried the meaning of *alien*, but later came to indicate a *spirit* or the *devil*. The kneeling person 㔾 (卩, R. 26), Adam, can be seen outside the garden 田 . He was now an *alien*. The couple are in *strange, unfamiliar* 異 28 (異) surroundings outside the garden. The upraised arms indicate worship. Adam and Eve, when turned out of the garden, were *alone* 單 29 (單). The conjoined couple ∞ are depicted outside the garden 田 .

Whereas Adam had previously loved to meet face-to-face with God, now he was filled with *fear, dread* 畏 30 (畏). God is represented by the tall person who prophesizes 卜 (卜, R. 25) the fate of Adam, the exiled *alien* 鬼 (鬼).

An additional meaning of 鬼 is "to return." According to the ancient interpretation, Confucius said in the *Book of Rites*, or the *Li Ji*:

Beginnings—Salvation

**Every creature will die, and when he dies,
he <u>returns</u> (鬼) to dust.**[31]

This was the fate pronounced by God upon the first couple, Genesis 3: 19:

*"For dust you are,
And to dust you shall <u>return</u>."*

Radical 203 (222)

黑 黑

Oracle bone Bronzeware Traditional Simplified

Definition: evil, dark, black, secret

Analysis: From the radical *evil, dark, black, secret* [32](黑) we learn that the result of the first *evil* deed was that the *noble* (大) persons were exiled from the *garden*. But there was to be a remedy for the *evil, blackness* (黑). The ancient sage, Lao Zi in his *Dao De Jing* wrote of the "Holy Man" to come. Surely this was Jesus Christ. Note this reference:

*[The Holy Man] knows the white [白],
but keeps the black [黑].*[33]

It may be universally true that black [黑] is often used to represent unrighteousness, and white [白] righteousness. When Adam and Eve sinned against God, they lost their "white" robe of righteousness and innocence, and put on the "black" clothes of unrighteousness and guilt. But the God of Heaven sent His Son to take on the blackness of the sinner, so that he might be clothed with the gloriously white righteousness of Christ.

*For He [God the Father] made Him [the Son]
who knew no sin to be sin [black]
for us, that we might become the righteousness
[white] of God in Him. (2 Corinthians 5: 21).*

The Beginning of Chinese Characters

Radical 169 (46)   門   門 门

Oracle bone Bronzeware Traditional Simplified

Definition: gate, door

Analysis: As Adam and Eve passed through the eastern garden *gate* 門 34 (門) they realized this meant exclusion from the life-giving tree of life and immortality. Note the hands 北 blocking the *gate* 門 entrance.

They could not go past the *gate* 門 (門) to eat from the *tree* 木 of life. There was a *barrier* 閑 35 (閑) due to the guarding cherubim angels. The *"flaming sword which turned in every direction"* (Genesis 3:24), made the gate area *fiery, glorious* 閃 36 (閃). Note the *fire* 火 (火, R. 86) at the gate. Could not this flashing sword actually represent God's glorious presence there at Eden's gate? In another Hebrew Scripture, God says, *"I will speak with you. . . from between the two cherubim. . ."* (Exodus 25:22). Also, of God, the Scriptures state, *"You [God] who dwell between the cherubim [angels], shine forth!"* (Psalm 80:1).

And so the garden gate at the eastern border of Eden became the new site where Adam and Eve came to commune with God. They came to *ask, inquire* 問 37 (問) of God concerning their needs. Notice the *mouth* 口 (口), indicating speaking. Their listening was represented by *listen, hear* 聞 38 (聞) with an *ear* 耳 (耳) at the *gate* 門 (門).

Radical 62 (101)   戈   戈 戈

Oracle bone Bronzeware Traditional Simplified

Definition: spear, lance, type of weapon

Beginnings—Salvation

Analysis: The radical *spear, lance* 丨 39 (戈) is used in many characters. In the character *to guard against, warn* 𠂇 40 (戒), the upraised worshiping *hands* 丫丫 of Adam and Eve at the gate of Eden where the flaming sword, *a type of weapon* 丨 (戈), *guarded against* 𠂇 (戒) the couple eating from the tree of life.

To guard the frontiers 忄 41 (戍) shows a *type of weapon* 丨 (戈) and a *person* 人 (angel) who *guards the frontier* 忄 (戍) of the garden of Eden. The first couple were prevented from becoming immortal sinners incurred by entering and eating from the tree of life, thus being protected from eternally suffering the miserable consequences of sin.

Radical 63

Oracle bone   Bronzeware   Traditional   Simplified

Definition: a door, to protect, stop

Analysis: The radical *door, to protect, stop* 戶 42 (户) reveals God's *hand* 彐 (爪, R. 87) at the "door" 丨 or at the Holy Mountain 厂 as seen in the *Shuo Wen* radical 437 戶 . In this seal character, "hand" 彐 here becomes a "person" 彐 . In one Seal character *door* 戶 43 (户), another feature of the Mount 厂 is found—a *tree* 木 , probably the tree of life to which the *door* of Eden was now closed.

The Bible symbolism for the *door* is interesting, for it may refer to Jesus Christ. In John 10: 9, Jesus proclaimed:

> "I am the <u>door</u>. If anyone enters by Me, he will be saved, and will go in and out and fine pasture."

In other words, Jesus is the entering way to eternal salvation.

Let us examine another character containing this radical: *to open, begin,*

The Beginning of Chinese Characters

lead the way, uncover 󰁋 44 (启) that depicts a *person* ⊌ whose *hand* 冫 opens the *door* 卩. Jesus also said in Revelation 3: 20:

> "Behold, I stand at the <u>door</u> and knock.
> If anyone hears My voice and <u>opens the door</u>,
> I will come in to him and dine with him,
> and he with Me."

Radical 145 (161)

Oracle bone   Bronzeware   Traditional   Simplified

Definition: clothes

Analysis: When Adam and Eve had presented themselves before God in the garden wearing fig-leaf coverings, He viewed them with mercy. God then expelled them from their Eden home, but He had a wonderful plan to save them from the death sentence incurred by their sin.

> *Also for Adam and his wife the LORD God made tunics of skin, and clothed them. (Genesis 3: 21).*

To make *clothes* 󰁋 45 (衤) of skins meant the death of animals to cover ⌒ (⼀ , R. 8) the sinful couple 󰁋 (actually one *person* ⼃ , the woman, is seen coming from the side of the first *person* ⼂ , Adam, 人 R. 9). The death of animals and use of their skins for clothing symbolized the death of Jesus Christ for Adam and Eve, with the resultant robe-gift of His righteous character.

God's provision of a change of *clothes* 󰁋 (衤) made from skins of sacrificed animals was meant to teach Adam and Eve that they needed to *rely on* 󰁋 46 (依) Him for hope of salvation from eternal death. Inserted into

168

Beginnings—Salvation

the *clothing* 衣 graph is the great *Person* 人 (人), God.

Innocent animals had *to die* 夅 47 (卒) by Adam's hand so that God could provide *clothes* 衣 for the sinful couple. Adam and Eve must have a *change* 爻 (爻, R. 89) of mind and heart and *"to be dead indeed to sin"*. (*Romans 6:11*). But unfortunately a *change* 爻 was also taking place in the relationship between Adam and Eve.

Radical 18 (27)

𠂌   刂 刀

Oracle bone   Bronzeware   Traditional   Simplified

Definition: a knife, razor

Analysis: The radical *knife, razor* 𠂌 48 (刀) appears in several Chinese characters to represent an instrument used for killing, or to represent death itself. When the Lord God made *clothing* 衣 (衤) of skins, a *knife* 𠂌 (刀) must be used to kill the sacrificial animals in order to *cover* 亠 (亠) the disobedient couple 人 (人). This was the *beginning* 初 49 (初) of the plan of salvation for humanity.

The result of their *perverse, wicked* 刺 (刺) behavior in eating with their *mouths* 口 fruit from the forbidden *tree* 木 (木), instead of *restraining* 束 (束) themselves, meant death as symbolized by a *knife* 𠂌 (刂).

Radical 93 (110)

Ψ   牛 牛

Oracle bone   Bronzeware   Traditional   Simplified

Definition: bullock, ox

The Beginning of Chinese Characters

Analysis: As well as sacrificing sheep, both the ancient Hebrew and Chinese peoples also sacrificed *bulls* 50 (牛). The character *sacrificial animals* , 51 (牢) shows *bulls* (牛) and *sheep* (羊) whose blood would flow as a *fountain* 52 (泉, see under R. 85), to wash away their sins. Notice that the lower part of both of these radicals , contain the "God symbol" (又, R. 29).

It was a *male animal* 53 (牡) that would die in the place of Adam, the first *mature male* ⊥ (士, R. 33) person. God the *Father* (父, R. 88) would send His Son, Jesus, to be the good *Shepherd* , 54 (牧). The Son, Jesus, was also represented by the sacrificial *bull* or *sheep* (羊). (See "Significance of the Sanctuary," Appendix II, p. 243 .)

Radical 31 (59)

Oracle bone   Bronzeware   Traditional   Simplified

Definition: an enclosure

Analysis: Again, there are no free-standing oracle bone or bronzeware renditions for this radical, but from its meaning, *enclosure* (囗), and the characters containing the graph, it appears that this refers to the Garden of Eden. Eden, with its fruit trees, was the first *orchard* 55 (圃), and could indeed be described as the garden *enclosure* (囗) given by the *Father* (甫 , see under R. 101).

The new site of worship at the eastern *gate* (門) of Eden is memorialized in the character *border, boundary* 56 (囲). God's Son, Jesus, who became a man, is represented in this graph by (大), a second *Noble* Man, while His legs are melded with the legs of the *disobedient* (㐄) first man, Adam. *"The first man was of the earth, made of dust; the second Man is the Lord from heaven." (1 Corinthians 15: 47)*. A worshiper is kneeling before the second Man [representing Jesus Christ] who has come to be the sacrifice for sins and take the place of the first

Beginnings—Salvation

disobedient man. The garden enclosure ▢ is also seen. This *border* 🐫 (囲), at the closed gate of Eden, is the reference for the Chinese Border Sacrifice. <u>The original Border Sacrifice was at the gate of the garden of Eden!</u>

Therefore, all people can *rejoice* and *give thanks to* 𠂇 [57] (幸) the Savior who came to die as a substitute for Adam and all *disobedient* ヤ (屰) mankind. Therefore, all people should *take hold of, grasp* 執 [58] (執) the Savior in order to be saved from eternal death. In this graph, the worshiper 乚 represents all sinners as well as Adam. This Border Sacrifice dates back over 4,000 years. We find that God, Himself gave this ceremony to the Chinese:

> **Tian [Heaven, God, 天] gave the pattern**
> **and the sage followed it.**
> **The Border Sacrifice is to manifest the**
> **Dao of Heaven.**[59]

[See Section III, R. 185, pp. 126, 127 for explanation of the Dao].

> **The bull is used as the sacrificial animal**
> **in the Border Sacrifice.**[60]

The Border Sacrifice, in fact, was looking forward to the crucifixion of Jesus <u>outside the gate</u> of Jerusalem many centuries later.

> *Therefore Jesus also, that He might sanctify the people*
> *with His own blood, <u>suffered outside the gate</u>.*
> *(Hebrews 13: 12).*

Through the blood of Christ, the closed gate of Eden, where the Border Sacrifice was memorialized for ages in China, will be opened again forever.

> *Blessed are those who do His commandments, that*
> *they may have the right to the tree of life, and may*
> *enter <u>through the gates</u> into the city.*
> *(Revelation 22:14, KJV).*

The Beginning of Chinese Characters

Radical 143 (181)

Oracle bone Bronzeware Traditional Simplified

Definition: blood, blood relationship

Analysis: The interesting radical *blood* 61 (血) shows the holy *flame* ◊ (﹅, R. 3) being poured into a *vessel* (皿 , R. 108) composed of two conjoined *persons* ↑ + ↑ (人), Adam and Eve. Notice how closely "blood and life" are connected. The Bible says, *"it [blood] is the life of all flesh."(Leviticus 17:14)* The blood (血) from the sacrificial animals symbolized Jesus' *holy* ◊ (﹅) blood that would wash away the sins of the whole world. *"...without shedding of blood there is no remission [forgiveness of sins]." (Hebrews 9: 22).*

In the figure, *blood* , we can also see the origin of the character, *Lord, Master* 62 (主), the God who would give His life *blood* ["shorthand" form].

Driven out of their lovely home in Eden, Adam and Eve must now build themselves a new dwelling place outside the gate. We read from

Genesis 4: 1-3:

> *Now Adam knew Eve his wife, and she conceived*
> *and bore Cain, and said, "I have gotten a man from*
> *the LORD."*
> *Then she bore again, this time his brother Abel.*
> *Now Abel was a keeper of sheep, but Cain was a tiller*
> *of the ground.*
> *And in the process of time it came to pass that Cain*
> *brought an offering of the fruit of the ground to the LORD.*

Cain brought a *"bloodless"* offering of fruit to present to the LORD. We will learn shortly of the direful result.

Beginnings—Salvation

Radical 191

鬥　斗

Oracle bone　Bronzeware　Traditional　Simplified

Definition: to fight, quarrel, contest, provoke

Analysis: *To fight, quarrel* 〈oracle〉 63 (鬥) shows two *persons* 〈figure〉 (人) with arms and *hands* 〈hand〉 (手) interlocked in a fight. This was yet another consequence of Adam and Eve's sin. No longer would they or their descendants live in perfect harmony, but *fighting* and *quarrelling* would enter all human relationships, as in today's world.

Genesis 4: 4, 5, 8-11, 15, 16:

> *Abel also brought of the firstlings of his flock and of their fat. And the LORD respected Abel and his offering, but He did not respect Cain and his offering. And Cain was very angry, and his countenance fell. . . .*
> *Now Cain talked with Abel his brother; and it came to pass, when they were in the field, that Cain rose against Abel his brother and killed him.*
> *Then the LORD said to Cain, "Where is Abel your brother?" And he said, "I do not know. Am I my brother's keeper?"*
> *And He said, "What have you done? The voice of your brother's blood cries out to Me from the ground. So now you are cursed from the earth, which has opened its mouth to receive your brother's blood from your hand. . . ."*
> *And the LORD said to him, "Therefore, whoever kills Cain, vengeance shall be taken on him sevenfold."*
> *And the <u>LORD set a mark on Cain</u>, lest anyone finding him should kill him.*
> *Then Cain went out from the presence of the LORD and dwelt in the land of Nod on the east of Eden.*

In these passages we find that Abel had presented the prophetic sheep sacrifice to God, and it was accepted. But note the rebellious spirit of Cain who, not only refused to comply with God's plan of redemption, and instead of giving the symbolic blood offering, presented God with fruit from his labor. When it was not accepted, he killed righteous Abel! This act of murder is recorded in the character *cruel, violent, fierce* 凶 64 (兇). Cain is pictured as the *elder brother* 兄 65 (兄) who is taking hold of his younger brother, Abel 大 (大). Note that there is a mark ╳ on Cain, as 兇, according to the Hebrew Scriptures above. How interesting too that *cruel and older brother* are both pronounced "xiong."

Radical 123 (157)

Oracle bone   Bronzeware   Traditional   Simplified

Definition: a sheep, goat

Analysis: We have just read that *"Abel brought of the firstlings of his flock and of their fat. And the LORD respected Abel and his offering."* (Genesis 4: 4). The *sheep* 羊 66 (羊), above all animals was to symbolize God's own Son, Jesus, for He was called *"the Lamb of God who takes away the sin of the world."* (John 1: 29).

In the character for *righteousness* 義 67 (義), we find the *sheep* 羊 (羊), like a garment, covering *me, I* 我 68 (我). But "I, me" is composed of a hand 手 holding a weapon, a *lance* 戈 69 (戈). This tells the story that if *I* 我 (我)repent and take a *lance* 戈 (戈) in my hand 手 and kill the sacrificial *sheep* 羊 (羊), then my sins can be forgiven [covered] and I can be declared *righteous* 義 (義) by God.

Originally it was Adam and Eve whose sins were covered by the skins of sheep, symbolizing the righteous, sinless Lamb of God. This is demonstrated in the character *beautiful* 美 70 (美), for the *noble* 大 (大) person [Adam or Eve] is portrayed as covered by a *sheep* 羊 (羊). When Jesus, the Lamb, covered their sins, they were indeed beautiful in God's eyes, for God saw only His sinless Son, symbolized by the sheep. Jesus' beautiful, sinless character was thus imputed to them while their sin was transferred to Him.

Radical 22 (15)

Oracle bone Bronzeware Traditional Simplified

Definition: a box, strong container

Analysis: From the character 匿 71 (匚), *to deliver*, it is clear that only the *Lamb* 羊 (羊), Jesus, is able to deliver us from punishment for our sins. We must be in Christ, who is like a *strong container* 匚 72 (匚), to be delivered. We cannot save ourselves. Only by asking Jesus into our lives as Lord and Savior can we be saved. The wise king, Solomon said:

> *The name of the LORD*
> *is a strong tower;*
> *The righteous run to it and are*
> *safe. (Proverbs 18: 10).*

Radical 23 (15)

Oracle bone Bronzeware Traditional Simplified

Definition: a box, to conceal, hide

Analysis: There are no free-standing oracle bone or bronzeware

The Beginning of Chinese Characters

renditions of the radical meaning *to hide*. ⌐ (⊏), However, in a character containing this radical, *place, area* 品 ⁷³ (區), three M*ouths*, *Persons* ⊽ (口 , see R. 30) are seen, indicating the Trinity, the Godhead. To avoid the punishment for sin, we must *hide, be concealed* ⌐ (⊏) in the only safe *place* 品 (區), in God's care.

Radical 50 (57)

Oracle bone   Bronzeware   Traditional   Simplified

Definition: a covering, piece of cloth

Analysis: Unfortunately the current definition of this radical, *a covering, piece of cloth* 巾 ⁷⁴ (巾) does not really fit, for the graph appears to be the lower end of the radical *tree* 木 (木, R. 75). Adam and Eve's need of a *covering* 巾 (巾) for their nakedness was the result of eating from the forbidden *tree* 木 .

We have also seen that it was God who provided garments made from animal skins to cover Adam and Eve's nakedness. To obtain these skins, a sacrifice of innocent animals had to be performed by Adam, the sinner. The death of these animals pointed to the coming Savior, Jesus Christ, who would take Adam's and our sins to the cross with Him, where He died.

Di (Shangdi), God 帝 (上帝 see under R. 30) was discussed in Section I under the very first radical. It is now appropriate for us to introduce another oracle bone rendition of *Di (Shangdi)* 帝 ⁷⁵ (上帝), for Shangdi <u>is</u> the original God of China!

An amazing prophetic revelation is contained within the ancient script of the name of China's God! We find three God radicals ⊢ + ⊤ + ⊣

(示 , R. 113), indicating the Godhead. The middle God radical 丅 clearly represents Jesus, the *perfect* │ (十) Person from *above* ═ (上). Jesus became a *man* 亻 (人), which is cleverly drawn into the character. He was *morally upright, the central focus, a pattern* 丼 (方, R. 70, p. 189). These definitions distinctly portray Jesus. Now superimpose 丅 and 丼 on the *tree* 朩 as 朩̄. Jesus was nailed to a tree, a wooden cross, whereby He became the *central focus* and completed God's redemptive plan for humanity. His cross became the tree of life for each of us:

> [Christ] who Himself bore our sins in His own
> body on the tree. (1 Peter 2: 24).

And this is not all! Because of Jesus' love for us, He became the *fuel used in sacrifices* ※ [76] (祭). His life was expended for us.

┌┬┐ + 亻 + 丼 + 朩 + ※ + ═ = 禾̄

Godhead   Man   morally upright   tree   fuel   above   Shangdi, God

The character, *Lamb* ᗰ (羔), relates the same story: the *Sheep* 羊 (羊 , R. 123) of God, Jesus, was represented as the fuel for the *fire* ᗰ (火) of the sacrifice.

Shangdi is none other than Jesus Christ, our God and promised Savior. The ancient Chinese Border Sacrifice pointed to the atoning death of Jesus on the cross for the sins of the world.

This loving Savior, Shangdi, pleads:

> "Turn to Me now and be saved,
> people all over the world!
> I am the only God there is.
>   (Isaiah 45 :22, TEV).

In a remarkable way, the beginnings of human life on planet earth; the Creator-God's original direct communication with man on the Holy Mount of Eden; the unfortunate beginning of disobedience and sin in the earth; the loving Creator's solution to man's death decree by the sacrifice of Himself— all has been faithfully recorded in the most primitive and basic elements— the radicals of the Chinese writing system. This would surely indicate that the original intent of the Chinese was to produce a hieroglyphic writing to store for posterity this sacred information.

But this is not all! There is yet additional information to be gleaned from the radicals— the actual topography of the Garden of Eden, so often considered "mythical." This garden, however, was a real place. Its features have been recorded not only in the pictographic Chinese characters, but also in many descriptive verses scattered throughout the Bible.

In the final Section VI, the Bible, amplified by pictographic Chinese characters, will draw what appear to be, exciting descriptive details of the long-lost Paradise of antiquity.

---

[1] Hung Pei Chiang, *Ching Wen P'ien Ching Wen* (Taipei: Kung I Publ. Co., 1974) No. 8.12. [Hereafter abbreviataed HPC].

[2] Lin Chih Ch'ing, *Ting Cheng Liu Shu T'ung* (Shanghai: Kuang-I Publ. Co., 1936), Sn. I, Part 2, p. 12. [Hereafter abbreviated LCC].

[3] LCC, Sn. VI, Part 14, p. 15.

[4] Ibid.

[5] Ibid.

[6] Ibid., p. 14.

[7] Chung-kuo K'e-hsueh-yuan k'ao-ku yen-chiu-so, *Chia-Ku Wen-Pien* (Peking: K'ao-ku-hsueh chuan-k'an yi-chung ti-shih-ssu hao, 1965), no. 13.3. [Hereafter abbreviated

CKWP].

8 CKWP, no. 13.4.
9 Ibid., no. 2.30.
10 ibid., no. 2.30.
11 Jin Gu Wen, *Zi Shuo Li* (Taiwan: An Guo Jun, 1983), p. 153. [Hereafter abbreviated ZSL].
12 HPC, no. 11.12.
13 ZSL, p. 33.
14 ZSL, p. 26.
15 CKWP, no, 6.5.
16 Ibid., no. 4.19.
17 ZSL, p. 59.
18 CKWP, no. 4.21.
19 Ma Wei Ching, *Wei Ching Chia Ku Wen Yuan* (Yunlin: Ma Fu Distributor, 1971), p. 792. [Hereafter abbreviated MWC].
20 Ibid., p. 793.
21 Bernhard Karlgren, *Grammata Serica, Script and Phonetics in Chinese* (Taipei: Ch'eng-Wen Publ. Co., 1966), p. 269, 270. [Hereafter abbreviated GS].
22 HPC, no. 5.37.
23 Ibid.
24 HPC. no. 13.13.
25 Ibid., no.13.13.
26 CKWP, no. 9.6.
27 HPC, no. 9.13.
28 MWC, p. 469.
29 CKWP, no. 2.14.
30 MWC, p. 504.
31 Wei Zhengtong, *The Wisdom of China* (Taipei: The Cowboy Publishing Co., Ltd., 1977), Vol. III, *Li Ji*, p. 699.

32 GS, p. 366.

33 Gia Fu Feng and Jane English, *Translation of Lao Tsu, Tao Te Ching* (Toronto: Vintage Books, Random House, Inc., 1989), Ch. 28, p. 30.

34 CKWP, no. 12.3

35 Chou Fa Kao, et al., *Ching Wen Ku Lin* (Hong Kong: Chinese University, 1975), p. 6566.

36 CKWP, no. 10.8.

37 Ibid., no. 2.8.

38 LCC, Sn. I, Part V, p. 10.

39 CKWP, no. 12.14.

40 MWC, p.835.

41 CKWP, no. 12.15.

42 MWC, p. 1226.

43 LCC, Sn, V, Part VI, p. 22.

44 GS, p. 274.

45 CKWP, no. 8.9

46 Ibid., no. 8.2.

47 HPC, no. 8.13.

48 CKWP, no. 4.22.

49 Ibid.

50 CKWP, no. 2.3.

51 Ibid., no. 4.14.

52 CKWP, no. 11.10.

53 CKWP, no. 2.4.

54 Ibid., no. 3..26.

55 MWC, p. 106.

56 CKWP, no. 10.15.

57 Ibid., no. 10.14

58 Ibid.

59 Wu Shuping, *The Four Books and Five Jing in Modern Chinese* (Beijing: International Cultural Publication, Inc., 1996). Vol. III, *Li Ji*, p. 554.

60 Ibid.

61 CKWP, no. 5.14.

62 ZSL, p. 70.

63 CKWP, no. 3.12.

64 MWC, p.504.

65 Ibid. p. 393.

66 CKWP, no. 4.13.

67 Ibid., no. 12.18.

68 Ibid.

69 Ibid., no. 12.14.

70 Ibid., no. 4.14.

71 MWC, p. 1283.

72 Ibid., p. 1044.

73 Ibid., p. 755.

74 Ibid., p. 1066.

75 CKWP, no. 1,2.

76 Ibid., no. 10.7.

The Beginning of Chinese Characters

Section VI

BEGINNINGS—
EDEN'S TOPOGRAPHY

Ethel R. Nelson

Great is the LORD, and greatly to be praised
In the city of our God, in His holy mountain.
Beautiful in elevation, the joy of the whole earth,
Is Mount Zion on the sides of the north.
The city of the great King. . .
Walk about Zion, and go all around her.
Count her towers; mark well her bulwarks;
(Psalm 48: 1,2, 12-13)

Beginnings—
Eden's Topography

The following 29 radicals have been difficult to place in this study—as well as the most unusual to interpret. However, these radicals are also perhaps the most interesting, as they appear to give pictorial hints as to the <u>actual topography</u> of the Garden of Eden! How is this possible? We must repeat the proposed chronology of the Chinese, stated in the Introduction.

About 101 years after the devastating flood of Noah's day, another event of great importance took place. In the fifth generation after Noah, we read of this incident:

> *To Eber [son of Salah, son of Arphaxad, son of Shem, son of Noah] were born two sons: the name of one was <u>Peleg, for in his days the earth was divided</u>.... (Genesis 10: 25).*

Evidently, at the time of the birth of this baby, the "earth was divided," and so Eber named his newborn son "Peleg," meaning "division." Thus we may ask, how was the earth "divided?" Again, we find the answer in the Bible:

> *These were the sons of Shem, according to their families, <u>according to their languages, in their lands,</u> according to their nations...and from these the <u>nations were divided on the earth after the flood</u> .(Genesis 10: 31, 32)*

It appears likely that the Chinese are descendants of Shem, one of Noah's three sons. Following the universal flood, the Chinese family was probably in close association with not only Shem, but also with Noah himself during the one hundred years between the flood and the time when the *"earth was divided according to languages."* It would seem that this following incident must have therefore instigated the great "division."

Genesis 11: 1-9:

> *Now the whole earth had one language and one speech.*
>
> *And it came to pass, as they [some of the descendants of Noah after the flood] journeyed from the east, that they found a plain in the land of Shinar, and they dwelt there.*
>
> *Then they said to one another, "Come, let us make bricks and bake them thoroughly." They had brick for stone, and they had asphalt for mortar.*
>
> *And they said, "<u>Come, let us build ourselves a city, and a tower whose top is in the heavens;</u> let us make a name for ourselves, lest we be scattered abroad over the face of the whole earth."*
>
> *But the LORD came down to see the city and the tower which the sons of men had built.*
>
> *And the <u>LORD said, "Indeed the people are one and they all have one language</u>, and this is what they begin to do; now nothing that they propose to do will be withheld from them.*
>
> *"<u>Come, let Us go down and there confuse their language</u>, that they may not understand one another's speech."*
>
> *So the LORD scattered them abroad from there over the face of all the earth, and they ceased building the city.*
>
> *Therefore its <u>name is called Babel, because there the LORD confused the language of all the earth; and from there the LORD scattered them abroad over the face of all the earth.</u>*

As men had begun to reproduce and repopulate the earth after the flood, four generations had passed, and there had arisen a large populace of rebellious people in the land of Shinar who were determined not to follow Noah, Shem, or their God. These were descendants of Noah's son, Ham. We read from

Genesis 10 : 6-10

> "*The sons of Ham were Cush, Mizraim, Put, and Canaan... Cush begot Nimrod; he began to be a mighty one on the earth. He was a mighty hunter before the LORD;... And <u>the beginning of his kingdom was Babel</u>, Erech, Accad, and Caineh, <u>in the land of Shinar.</u>*"

The Lord thwarted the building plans of Nimrod at Babel by confusing their language. The result was a mass migration, according to language groups, over the face of the earth. The Chinese doubtless took part in this migration, moving their great family eastward at this date, c2247 B.C., calculated from the genealogical record of Genesis 11. Compare the date of the first Chinese dynasty —2205 B.C.—only 42 years later!

The defiant groups, still possessing a rebellious spirit, evidently determined to build their cities and towers elsewhere. Thus we find a proliferation of similar pagan temple-towers widespread around the world. Wrote George Stanley Faber (1773-1854), of the Church of England, in 1815: "The various systems of Pagan Idolatry in different parts of the world correspond so closely... that they cannot have been struck out independently in the several countries where they have been established, but must have all originated from some common source."[1] That common source, it would seem, is the original Tower of Babel. Further comment on this thesis will be made at the end of the Section.

As we have learned, the Chinese forebears, who likely migrated from the Babel site in 2247 B.C. eastward to the land which would become China, were firm believers in the Creator-God of Noah, and therefore recipients of accurate antediluvian history. Noah's father, Lamech was 56 years old when Adam died at the age of 930 years. Consequently, the early Chinese believers were in a position to obtain direct word-of-mouth detailed revelations regarding the beauties of the original paradise of God on earth, the Garden of Eden.

Therefore, in order to preserve this unusual knowledge, after the confusion of languages at Babel, perhaps even God Himself inspired the faithful Chinese ancestors to include descriptive pictograms of Eden in their new writing system. Thus a most unusual opportunity was used to store and perpetuate this knowledge—for more than 4,000 years!

In the chapter on the worship practices of Adam and his wife (Section III), we found them climbing a Holy Mountain to meet with God face-to-face for communion and instruction. Now, let us retrieve more specific details of the ancient earth's most holy meeting place—Eden's Holy Mountain. We shall consider the pictographic, "archaeological" details of this original sanctuary, as recorded in the final 29 ancient Chinese radicals to be studied. It should be stated that many of the pictograms are metaphorical with a double interpretation: possibly an actual, physical site, as well as a symbolic representation of the Creator-Godhead.

The Holy Bible also abounds with the same type of scattered metaphorical references to the real site and structure of both an earthly and a heavenly Holy Mountain [see Appendix I, "My Holy Hill"], so it appears that all of these Chinese pictograms convey the same ideas as the Bible.

Radical 70 (85)

丼　ㄏ　方　方

Oracle bone　Bronzeware　Traditional　Simplified

Definition: square, morally pure, center, place, plan

Analysis:

⊢ + ⊤ + ⌐ + ⼅ = 丼

God　God　God　Person　morally pure, square, center, place

The Godhead is here portrayed as *morally pure, square, central* 丼, ㄏ [2] (方). The first oracle bone symbol is apparently composed of three "God radicals" ⊢ + ⊤ + ⌐ (示, R. 113). The bronzeware figure ㄏ [3] (方), representing God, is quite remarkable in that it may be stretched out as ⼌, to represent the Holy Mount, which must have been a *central,* holy *place*.

In the character *to travel* [4] (旅), the mount is represented by ⼌, while Ψ depicts God on the mount. The two traveling *persons* (人) portray Adam and his wife approaching the Holy Mount. They often *returned* [5] (旋) to this *square, central, place* ⼌, depicted by the symbol for *rest, stop* [6] (止, R. 77).

In considering the Holy Mount a *square, central, place*, one might be inclined to consider a cubical shape with dimensions (length, width and height) equal. However another geometric figure also fulfills these measurements: an equilateral pyramid with square base and equivalent height. A pyramid has a shape more consistent with a mountain also. So let us consider the holy mountain in terms of a pyramid. But remember that the holy *moun-*

The Beginning of Chinese Characters

tain ▲▲▲ has three peaks, the middle peak being the highest.

It would seem that God often deals architecturally in "squares." Note the dimensions of the celestial Holy City, the New Jerusalem:

> *And the city is laid out as a square, and its length is as great as its breadth. . . .Its length, breadth, and height are equal.*
> *(Revelation 21: 16)*

But this is not all. After Moses led the Israelite escape from Egyptian bondage, God instructed him to build a portable sanctuary in the wilderness based upon squares. The "square arrangement" applied also to the surrounding Israelite encampment. (See Appendix II, "Significance of the Sanctuary," p. 243).

Why should an oracle bone radical meaning *square, central, place* 大 (方) be a pictogram of God himself with arms upraised? Apparently, God is personified in the high *central, square, place* of worship—the "sanctuary" to which Adam and his wife traveled daily to meet face-to-face with Him. Other radicals also clearly personifying God as the Holy Mountain are Radicals 112, 148, 125 and 168. This loving Creator-God has always wanted to be with mankind. The first couple could say:

> *"A glorious high throne from*
> *the beginning*
> *Is the place of our sanctuary."*
> *(Jeremiah 17: 12).*

We will next examine several of the metaphorical radicals describing the highest, central peak of the holy *mountain* ▲▲▲ (山 , R. 46) which portrays God (actually Jesus Christ) Himself.

Radical
112 (136)

      厂ㅂ   石   石

Oracle bone Bronzeware Traditional Simplified

Definition: rock, stone

Analysis:

      厂 + ㅂ = 厂ㅂ

      hill   mouth   Rock

As we examine the radical *Rock* 厂ㅂ [7] (石), we might ask first of all why "Rock" is capitalized. Throughout the Bible, the name of Jesus Christ is always capitalized, and He is often referred to as the "Rock." Note the several meaningful metaphors in this Psalm:

> *The LORD is my <u>rock</u> and my*
> *fortress and my deliverer:*
> *My God, my <u>strength,</u>*
> *in whom I will trust;*
> *My <u>shield</u> and the <u>horn of my</u>*
> *<u>salvation,</u> my <u>stronghold.</u>*
> *(Psalm 18: 2)*

For a full explanation of this radical, *Rock* 厂ㅂ , examine *hill* 厂 (厂 , R. 27). The *mouth* ㅂ (口) may refer to the Lord's Creatorship, *"by the breath of His mouth" (Psalm 33: 6)*. The radical *Rock* 厂ㅂ can also be interpreted as God's *mouth* ▽ communing with a *person* ㅂ (口), (Adam) on the summit of the "Rock."

When Moses led two million Hebrews out of Egyptian slavery, about 1445 B.C., through the wastes of the Sinai desert, they ran out of water. The Lord, who followed in a covering cloud, commanded Moses,

The Beginning of Chinese Characters

> "Behold, I will stand before you there on the rock in Horeb [Mt. Sinai] and you shall <u>strike the rock</u>, and water will come out of it, that the people may drink." (Exodus 17: 6).

> *He opened the rock,*
> *and water gushed out*
> *It ran in the dry places like a*
> *river. (Psalm 105: 41).*

This event of striking the Rock was a "type" [prophesy] of the death of Jesus, the mighty Rock, on the cross of Calvary. After He died,

> *One of the [Roman] soldiers pierced His side with a spear,*
> *and immediately blood and <u>water came out</u>. (John 19: 33, 34).*

This water was symbolic of the "water of life"—everlasting life and salvation which the death of Jesus for repentant sinners would bring. How does Eden's Holy Mountain bear out this symbolism, according to the Chinese radical pictograms? We must next examine the "water" radical.

Radical 85 (40, 125)   水   水

Oracle bone   Bronzeware   Traditional   Simplified

Definition: water

Analysis: Throughout the Bible, water is used as a metaphor to represent everlasting life. The first *water* [8] [9] (水) of life was found in the Garden of Eden. In the bronzeware, the Chinese represented *water* as being sacred (note the "blackening"). In fact, the character *eternal* [10] (永) depicts *water* surrounding a *Person [God]*, even as the symbolic "water of life" poured from the Rock in the Sinai desert, and water

Beginnings—Eden's Topography

gushed from Jesus' rent side after His death. Earlier, Jesus had said to a woman drawing water from a well:

> *Whoever drinks of the water that I shall give him will never thirst. But the water that I shall give him will become in him a fountain of water springing up into everlasting life."*
> (John 4: 13, 14).

Note the *river* � (川 , R. 47) in the character *deep, abyss* 〰 [11] (淵). This pictogram appears to be an illustration for the point of origin of the water of the River of Life. We will refer to this again when discussing Radical 106.

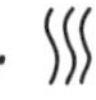

Radical 47 (78)

Oracle bone   Bronzeware   Traditional   Simplified

Definition: river, streams, to flow

Analysis: You will recall that the *garden* ⊞ (田 , R. 102) had a river flowing from its center outward in four directions. Both oracle bone and bronzeware figures for *river*  , 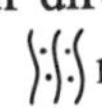 [12] , [13] (川) are significant in that they portray the Godhead. In  we find three *flames of fire* (ヽ , R. 3); in the figure  , we find the "blackening" consistent with holiness.

In one form of the "God radical" [14] (示 , R. 113), we discover that the source of the *river* was God Himself.

> *And he showed me a pure <u>river of water of life,</u> clear as crystal <u>proceeding from the throne of God</u> and of the Lamb. In the middle of its street, and on either side of the river, was the tree of life, . .*
> (Revelation 22: 1, 2)

Although this is a description of heaven, where God's throne is located, the Holy Mount of Eden must have been similar where the first couple met with God on the highest peak, the "Rock," of the Holy *Mountain* 🏔. Revelation tells us that a "street" as well as the river proceeded from the throne of God. Therefore, on the very top of this middle peak should be a large, flat, square area where the first couple came to worship God. Note too that in heaven there is not only a river of life, but also a tree of life spanning the river, similar to the tree of life in the middle of the earthly Garden of Eden. Then, as the river of life left this topmost, flat area, it must have cascaded down the slope of the tallest peak. All of this would lead us to believe that the Garden of Eden was indeed a miniature of heaven.

One derived character from this *river* radical, *a place surrounded by water, an islet* 〣 [15] (州), becomes very important as we proceed to determine the topography of Eden's Holy Mountain. You will note in the character *islet* 〣, is the symbol ◊ indicating holy, *flame* (丶 , R. 3). It would appear that the Rock, the central highest peak where God's throne is located, becomes an island, surrounded by water from the "river of life."

> *There is a river whose streams*
> *shall make glad the city of God,*
> *The holy place of the*
> *tabernacle of the Most High..*
> *God [the Rock] is in the midst of her,*
> *she shall not be moved;*
>   *(Psalm 46: 4, 5).*

Putting these metaphors together, we are led to conclude that the "Rock," the central highest peak of the Holy Mountain, also represents "the City of God," and is surrounded by water as an island.

Radical 106 (150)

Oracle bone Bronzeware Traditional Simplified

Definition: white, clear, pure, righteous

Analysis: Upon examining the ancient forms of *white, clear, pure* ⊖ 16 ⌣ 17 (白), especially the bronzeware, ⌣, one wonders how this pictogram represents *white, clear*. Actually, the radical ⌣ appears to be a *speaking* ⊟ mouth (compare 曰, R. 73), as well as the Holy *Mountain* ⌣ (山 , R. 46). Could the definition be derived from the white foam of a *fountain, spring* 𤽄 18 (泉) rising up in a geyser atop the Holy Mountain? Note the *water* ⺡ (水 , R. 85) flowing from *God* 丅 (示 , R. 113). Compare these verses from the Bible:

> And You [God] give them drink from
> the river of Your pleasures.
> For with You is <u>the fountain of life;</u>
> In Your light we see light.
> (Psalm 36: 8, 9).

From the character ⌣, it would seem that the *fountain* 𤽄 was located on the Holy Mount and is symbolic of God, the Creator of all, and the source of the river of life. Could the origin of the Fountain and the River be the *abyss, deep* 𣶒 (淵)?

Radical 51

Oracle bone Bronzeware Traditional Simplified

The Beginning of Chinese Characters

Definition: a shield, offend against

Analysis: The oldest pictograms (oracle bone) for *shield* 甶, 甴 19 (干) are indeed interesting. The configuration 甶 appears to have two bowing *persons* 川 (人, R. 9) standing on a *square, place, center* 口 (方, R. 70). This would, it seems, be a flat, *square, place* in the *center* of the Garden of Eden, on the top of the highest peak of the Holy Mountain (see previous discussion under R. 47).

In the bronzeware, this radical *shield* 丫 20 (干) becomes, significantly, the Great Unity, the Godhead 丫 (一, R. 1), and also the high *tower*. Thus, as we compare Psalm 18: 2 once more, we find that the *Shield* and *High Tower* are likewise metaphors for Jesus Christ, The *Rock* 㘣 (石, R. 112).

> *The LORD is my rock, and my*
> *fortress and my deliverer:...*
> *My buckler [shield] and the horn of*
> *my salvation, and my high tower.*
> (Psalm 18: 2, KJV).

Radical 148 (201)

  角 角

Oracle bone Bronzeware Traditional Simplified

Definition: horn, corner, angle

Analysis: First, let us quote still once again Psalm 18:2 that delineates significant, prophetic, symbolic, metaphors for Jesus Christ:

> *The LORD is my rock, and my*
> *fortress and my deliverer;*
> *My God, my strength,* ↙ *(R. 19)*

196

> *In whom I will trust;*
> *My <u>shield</u> and the <u>horn</u> of my salvation,*
> *my stronghold [<u>high tower</u>, KJV].*

The *horn* ⟨ [21] and ⟨ [22] (角) figures are similar, except that the bronzeware symbol ⟨ incorporates a *Person* ⟨ (人, R. 9), God [Jesus Christ] in the *Horn* (see R. 25). The *Shuo Wen* radical ⟨ depicts the *Person* even more clearly. Note that the *Horn* is also a high *Tower* in the above Psalm [King James Version]. So now we find that the *Rock* ⟨ (R. 112); the *Strength* ⟨ (R. 19); the *Shield* ⟨ (R. 51); and the *Horn* ⟨ represent the "High Tower" or middle peak of the Holy *Mountain* ⟨⟨ (山, R. 46). Even today, we find mountain peaks called "horns"—such as the Matterhorn.

But why should this Psalm call Jesus Christ the "Horn of Salvation?" Millennia after the Garden of Eden and before Jesus was born to the virgin, Mary, the priest Zacharias, prophesied:

> *Blessed is the Lord God of*
>   *Israel,*
> *For He has visited and*
>   *redeemed His people*
> *And has raised up <u>a horn of*
>   *salvation</u> for us,*
> *In the house of His servant*
>   *David.*   (Luke 1: 68, 69).

Jesus was that mysterious *Horn of Salvation* promised to the psalmist King David, ancestor of Mary, so many centuries before.

> *For the LORD has chosen [Mount]Zion;*
> *He has desired it for His habitation. . .*
> *There I will make <u>the horn of David</u>*
>   *to grow;. . . (Psalm 132: 13, 17).*

The Beginning of Chinese Characters

Familiar within the Hebrew sanctuary and temples were the "horned altars"—the bronze altar in the courtyard, and the altar of incense in the holy place (see Appendix II, "Significance of the Sanctuary"). In vision, the Hebrew prophet Ezekiel described a special altar:

The altar ["Harel"] hearth is four cubits high, with four horns extending upward from the hearth [Ariel]. (Ezekiel 43: 15).

"Harel" means "the mountain of God!" Therefore, the horned altars were miniatures of God's Holy mountain, with its four horns representing the four lower peaks (Figure 1). But where is the "Horn of Salvation?" On the center of the hearth [Ariel] was the place where the Lamb was sacrificed. "Ariel" has two meanings. According to Isaiah 29: 1,2, it represents Jerusalem, "the city where David dwelt" (therefore, subsequently, the New Jerusalem). But it also means "the Lion of God"—who is none other than Jesus Christ (Revelation 5: 5,6: "Lion of the tribe of Judah, the Root of David,").

Jesus, that "Horn of Salvation," the central "high tower,"would ultimately save all from their sins who believe in Him. How beautiful and meaningful are both the Chinese and Hebrew metaphors!

Radical 7 (11)

Oracle bone   Bronzeware   Traditional   Simplified

Definition: two, the second, above

Analysis: Here is a radical that carries different character equivalents in the oracle bone and bronzeware writing! In the oracle bone, ＝ [23] (二) indicates *two*; while ━ [24] (上) means *above*. The bronzeware ━ [25] (上) means only *above*.

Beginnings—Eden's Topography

The symbol *above* 二 (上) we have found in a number of characters, such as: *beginning* 亓 (元, see under R. 10); *Heaven, God* 天 (天, R. [90]); *to manifest,* "God radical" 丅 (示, R. 113); and *rain* 雨 (雨, R. 173). All of these characters represent God who comes down from *above* 二 (heaven).

This radical as *two, the second, above* 二 (上) is used, and has real significance in the following radical [168], meaning *second in excellence, inferior* 十 , 田 , as we shall learn.

Radical [168]

十 田 亞 亚

Oracle bone Bronzeware Traditional Simplified

Definition: second in excellence, inferior

Analysis: The character *second in excellence, inferior* 十 26 田 27
(亞) will take on special import as we further study the topography of the Holy Mountain, and will become increasingly clear and relevant as we study the next several radicals.

A figure found in a bronzeware dictionary with no accompanying contemporary character transliteration or meaning is 跽 28 , but obviously this tells us that the place, *secondary in excellence* 十 was a place of worship where two persons 跽 , on bended knee, have their hands upraised in adoration.

Another oracle bone character, *to resemble, be like, conform to* 若 29 (若) certainly portrays a worshipping figure 若 on bended knee with arms upraised to God 丫 (see discussion of 田 under R. 101) . The symbol 丫 is found within the 若 figure in the bronzeware 若 , thus further confirming that 十 is a Holy Place. This suggests that there are

199

The Beginning of Chinese Characters

actually two sites on the Holy Mountain where God is worshipped. It would seem that the place, being "second in excellence" and "inferior" is an area below the highest peak where God's throne and the source of the river of life are located. We might also ponder the unusual shape of the radical *second in excellence, inferior* 十 田 . The answer lies in the next R.144.

Radical 144

亻 ㄅㄴ 行

Oracle bone Bronzeware Traditional Simplified

Definition: a crossroad, to walk, travel

Analysis: This radical, and several characters containing it, will bring together important clues in solving Eden's Holy Mountain mystery. First, we'll examine the *crossroad, to walk* 亻 [30] ㄅㄴ [31] (行). The bronzeware ㄅㄴ does indeed look like a *crossroad*. But when we examine the character derivative *to overflow, to spread out, a lake, pond, beautiful* 衍 [32] 衍 [33] (衍), we find a *river* 巛 , 川 (川 , R. 47) flowing into the "crossroad," *spreading out* and making it a *beautiful lake* 衍 . Recall now that the Rock, Horn, High Tower became an *islet* 巛 (州 , see R. 47) from the waters of the river of life flowing around it, forming a lake.

Another radical that we've just examined comes to mind. There's the bronzeware 田 , 十 (亞 , R. [168]), meaning *second in excellence, inferior*. We might question: second or inferior to what? Observe that the center of 十 has a smaller square [see under the previous R. (168)] . Could this be an elevated, central, superior place of primary excellence?

Let's look again at one of the depictions of the radical, *mountain* ♛ (山 , R. 46). Observe again that the central peak, or *horn* 角 (角 , R. 148), is higher. We have already found that a *river* 巛 flows from the center of the *garden* ⊞ (田 , R. 102). This river flows from *a place surrounded by water, an islet* 〦 (州 , see R. 47), with the *source* 〦 (原 , see R. 27) of the river being a *fountain* 〦 (泉) that erupts from *the deep, abyss* 〦 (渊). This brings us full circle to another ancient form of the same character, *abyss* 〦 [34] (渊), that also displays the "God radical" 丁 in the center. Once again, it would surely seem that the "high Tower," the "Horn," the "Rock," is the island surrounded by water flowing from the river of life and forming a lake on the mountain, which, in turn, distributes water by four rivers from the four sides of the Holy Mountain.

Now it's time to solve the mystery by going to the Bible. The book of Revelation reveals a heavenly "Garden of Eden" with a river of life, and the tree of life. Revelation 14: 1-3 describes a Holy Mountain, Mount Zion, and a scene that will help delineate the Eden topography:

> "Then I looked, and behold, a Lamb *standing on Mount Zion,* and with Him one hundred and forty-four thousand... And I heard the sound of harpists playing their harps. And they sang as it were a new song *before the throne.*"

Then read the following verses from Revelation 15: 2, 3:

> "And I saw something like a *sea of glass mingled with fire,* and those who have the victory... *standing on the sea of glass,* having the harps of God. And they sing the song of Moses, the servant of God, and the song of the Lamb, ..."

Here is a heavenly scene featuring victorious persons "redeemed from the earth" (Revelation 14: 3) who stand on Mount Zion, singing before the throne, standing on the sea of glass. The sea of glass is therefore pictured as being on the holy Mount Zion, a place *second in excellence* 〦 (亞), *inferior* to the throne that is on the high middle tower of the mountain. From this lofty central peak, the *river* 𝕵 of life flows from God's throne, being fed from the *fountain* 𝕽 (泉 , under R. 106) of life. In the earthly Garden of Eden, both *trees* 𝕏𝕏 (木 , R. 75), the Tree of Life and the Tree of the Knowledge of Good and Evil, were also located in the middle of the garden, therefore on the central high peak. Recall the character *burning* 𝕎 (焚 , see R. 46).

Picture, then, the river flowing <u>down</u> from the central, elevated peak, and spreading out to form the "sea of glass" that surrounds the central peak, making it an "island." Now the question arises: since the mountain pictograms always show three peaks, how can water be contained on the top of the mountain with just three peaks? It can't! <u>There should be five peaks.</u> The great central peak (horn) is surrounded by <u>four peaks (horns) on the four corners of the mountain.</u> This would also explain why the radical *horn* 𝔸 (角 , R. 47) also means *corner!* (See proposed "Holy Hill" Figures 1a & 1b).

> *Therefore thus says the Lord God:*
> *"Behold, I lay <u>in Zion</u> a stone*
> *for a foundation,*
> *A tried stone, a precious*
> *<u>cornerstone</u>, a sure*
> *foundation;*
>   *(Isaiah 28: 16).*

> *A stone which the builders*
> *rejected*
> *Has become the chief*
> *<u>cornerstone [capstone]</u>,*
>   *Psalm 118: 22, NIV].*

If one viewed the Holy Mountain from any of its four sides, one would see only three peaks—just as the pictogram *mountain* 𝕄 portrays.

By now, we can visualize a four-sided, glorious mountain rising up like an equilateral pyramid. Part way to the top, however, at the four corners are lower "horned" peaks. The horns at the four corners explain the indentations and peculiar shape of the *lake* ⌐⧙⌐ , the "sea of glass." The *island* ⧙⧙ , the central, tallest peak, [the *Rock,* the *"Capstone,"* the *Horn*], rises higher. From the four sides of the "sea of glass" on the mountain, descend the four branches of the river of life, nicely pictured by the radical *garden* ⊞ .

But perhaps the best biblical support for the envisioned Holy Mountain is found in Ezekiel's description of a "stepped" horned altar in Ezekiel 43: 13-17. The top of the altar is described:

> *"The altar hearth is four cubits high, with <u>four horns extending upward from the hearth.</u>*
> *The altar hearth is twelve cubits long, twelve wide, square at its four corners;" (Ezekiel 43: 15, 16).*

From the description in Ezekiel, we can draw a three-stepped, horned altar (see Figure 1, and discussion under R. 148). But most interesting is the marginal interpretation of this "altar" that has a name—"Harel," meaning "the mountain of God!" So we may conclude that the horned altars found in the Hebrew sanctuary and temples were actually miniature replicas of God's Holy Mountain—the first earthly Holy Mountain being found in the Garden of Eden. But, we might ask, where is the central *"high tower, the horn of salvation"* on the horned altars? The lamb sacrifice placed in the center of the altar of sacrifice represented the Rock, the Horn of Salvation, the Shield—Jesus Christ, the *"Lamb slain from the foundation of the world." (Revelation 13: 8)* See also: Appendix I, "My Holy Hill," p. 235.

Now we have a number of additional radicals to complete this study of Eden's Holy Mountain topography.

Radical 156 (189)

大　彳止　走　走

Oracle bone　Bronzeware　Traditional　Simplified

Definition: to walk, run, go swiftly, travel

Analysis: The pictogram *to walk, run, go swiftly* 大 ³⁵ 彳止 ³⁶ (走) shows not only a person (Adam or his wife) going quickly with arms swinging, but also, in the bronzeware 彳止, reveals the site of destination 彳 on the Holy Mount. The goal is the "Sea of Glass," the *crossroad* 彳亍 (行, R. 144) on the holy Mount, a first stop on the way to visit with God at the peak. Compare also *second in excellence* 亞 [亞, (R. 168)]; *a small step* 彳 (彳, R. 60); *a long walk* 辶 (辵, R. 54); and *valley, hollow, ravine* 谷 (谷, R. 150).

Radical 76 (120)

𣥺　　　欠　欠

Oracle bone　Bronzeware　Traditional　Simplified

Definition: lacking, short of, deficient

Analysis: In studying the meaning of this radical, *lacking, short of* 𣥺 ³⁷ (欠), we ask, "short of or lacking" what? From the various characters formed from this radical, it becomes apparent that it is a *place* which is "short of" the final destination on the Holy Mount. Let us first examine a character with many meanings: *lower, inferior, a halting place, an interval, in the midst, stop for a rest, lower, inferior, in the midst* 仒 ³⁸ 次 ³⁹ (次)—all of which suggest the "sea of glass" (see 亞,

R. [168]), which is part way to the top of the Holy Mount, but is *lower, inferior, in the midst* 𖢅 (次). Note that Adam, the first man ᛈ (儿, R. 26), is accompanied by another *person* D (口, R. 30), his wife. They have paused at this *place in the midst* of the mountain. The *"breath"* 𖢅 𖢅 emitted from the couple is best explained in the next character as songs of praise.

Besides resting a bit at this *beautiful* 𖢅 (術, R. 144) place, Adam also spends his time in *singing* with *praises* and *chants* 𖢅 ⁴⁰ (歌). The glory of both the man 𖢅 and his wife is represented by the *sun* ☉ (日, R. 72), as they join in song.

Radical 180 (210)

𖢅　𖢅　音　音

Oracle bone　Bronzeware　Traditional　Simplified

Definition: a sound, tone, musical note

Analysis: In studying the previous R. 76, we found a character derivative, *to sing, chant, praise* 𖢅 (歌), where both Adam, as the man 𖢅 and his wife took part in singing praise. In this present character, *tone, musical note* 𖢅 ⁴¹ 𖢅 ⁴² (音), *we find a symbol nearly identical to word* 𖢅 (言, R. 149). To understand the connection, we must again go to the radical *bitter* 𖢅 (辛, R. 160), which we interpreted as the *second Noble Man* 𖢅 , Jesus Christ, who came down 𖢅 *from heaven above* 二 (上) as a human to suffer *bitterness* 𖢅 on behalf of mankind. Therefore, this time, in *musical note* 𖢅 (音), it appears to be Jesus who is represented as singing.

In the seal writing of *tone, musical note* 𖢅 ⁴³ (音), we find that the

205

The Beginning of Chinese Characters

singing mouth ᗡ takes the form of the Holy Mount ᐱ (山, R. 46). So, when the man ⅄ (卩, R. 26) reaches the *midpoint* ᗞ (次, see R. 76), the "sea of glass," in his climb to commune with God, he appears to be joined in song by Jesus! The "sea of glass" seems to be the site for singing:

> And I saw something like a sea of glass mingled with fire, and those who have the victory. . .standing on the sea of glass, having harps of God. And they sing the song of Moses. . . and the Lamb. . . . (Revelation 15: 2, 3).
>
> The LORD your God in your midst,
> The Mighty One, will save;. . .
> <u>He will rejoice over you with
> singing</u>;(Zephaniah 3: 17).

Radical 77 (102)

ᙏ   止   止

Oracle bone   Bronzeware   Traditional   Simplified

Definition: to stop, rest, come to arrive at

Analysis: As we study this radical, *to stop, rest, arrive at, come to* ᙏ , ᙏ [44] (止), we may conclude that the *foot* ᙏ , ᙏ belongs to Adam or his wife.

First, let us examine *just, pure, virtuous, original* 뮤 [45] 止 [46] (正), that pictures attributes consistent for Adam and the woman who were made in the image of *Tian, Heaven, God* ᛤ , ᚴ (天 , R. 113).

Let us also consider the character, *a step, a pace, to follow in the footsteps of* ᙏᙏ [47] (步). We find this symbol in the character *to ascend, proceed* [48] (陟) depicting a person's feet proceeding up the Holy

206

Mount 𖥂 (阝 , R. 170). In addition, the character *to wade a stream, pass through*〰️ , ≋ *49* (涉) illustrates the feet of the first man (or woman) wading through the waters of the River 〰️ of Life (on the Mount).

Radical 60 (62)

ㄏ　　　彳　彳

Oracle bone　Bronzeware　Traditional　Simplified

Definition: a step to the left, a small step

Analysis: To learn the true meaning of this radical, *a small step* ㄏ (彳), we will have to see how it is used in various characters as the radical is not free-standing. In *to move one's abode, migrate* 𢓊 *50* (徙), we find Adam or his wife *arriving* 𣥂 (止 . R. 77) at Eden's Holy Mountain, symbolized by ㄏ (the left half of ⼮⼯, see R. 144).

Another example, *to depart, go toward* 土 *51* 徃 *52* (往) shows Adam, the man of *clay, earth* 𛀁 (土 , R. 30), *resting, stopping* 𣥂 (止) as he *goes toward* 土 the Holy Mountain. In this bronzeware figure 徃 , we find the left half of ⼮⼯(行 , R. 144), indicating the place on the Holy Mount where the man is going to commune with the *King* 王 (王 , R. 96).

In *follow, obey* 𠔏 *53* (從), the ㄏ again depicts the left part of ⼮⼯(行 , R. 144). This time there are two *persons* 𠔼 (人 , R. 9) who have arrived on the Mount, at the "crossroad," the place of "secondary excellence, inferior," the biblical "sea of glass," on the way to their final meeting place at God's throne on the summit of the middle highest peak.

207

Radical 54

彳 亍   廴

Oracle bone Bronzeware Traditional Simplified

Definition: to move on, a long walk

Analysis: This radical 彳, 彳亍 (廴) is really identical to the radical meaning *a crossroad, to walk, travel* 彳亍 (行 , R. 144), and portrays the division of the four rivers from the "sea of glass" on the Holy Mount (see Radicals 102, 7, 47, 85, 144, 77, and 60). It is amazing how many references to this configuration are used, in the radicals alone!

To extend, spread, lengthen, invite 彳止 [54] (延) pictures a long walk for Adam to either the extension and spreading of the rivers, or to the site of forking of the rivers on the Holy Mount.

Even in the radical, *walking* 彳止 [55] (辶 , R. 162), the same site of the forking of the rivers is used as the place of walking to or from. So important was this place for a daily *walk* 彳止 by the first couple, that the site has forever been memorialized in this radical!

Radical 17 (38)

∪   凵 凵

Oracle bone Bronzeware Traditional Simplified

Definition: a receptacle

Analysis: Since there is again no free-standing oracle bone or bronzeware symbol for this radical, we must examine characters containing it, such as *to produce, beget, happen, appear* 凵,  [56] (出). At this place ∪ , a person ᗛ has been *begotten* and is *stopped, resting* ᗜ (止 , R. 77). Where is this place? The second character 彳止, makes clear

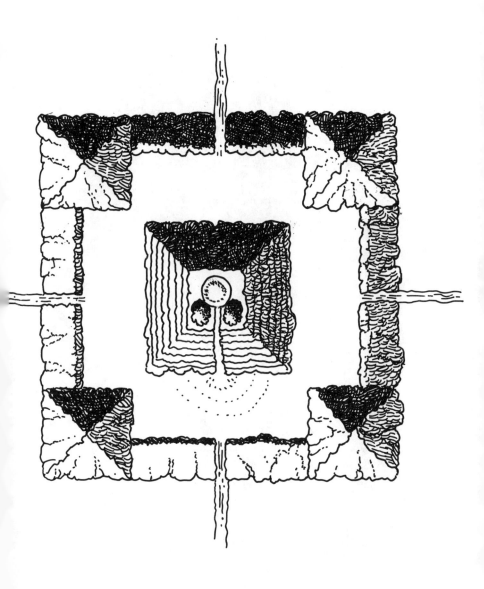

Figure 1a

Figure 1b

that the site is at the *crossroad* ⼅ ⼦ on the Holy Mountain.

Is it possible that this person is Adam, the first man 𠂉 (⼙ , R. 26), and that God has *aided, assisted* ⼼ [57] (函) in lifting the man from the earth in his creation? The *Shuo Wen* is even more specific regarding the site 㞢 [58] (函). The man ⼘ is arising from the central tower of the Holy *Mountain* ⼭ (⼭ . R. 46), the Rock, assisted by God's hands ⼌⼌.

> *[The LORD God said]:*
> *"Listen to Me, you who*
> *follow after*
> *righteousness,*
> *You who seek the LORD:*
> *Look to the rock from which*
> *you were hewn,*
> *And to the hole of the pit*
> *From which you were dug.*
> *(Isaiah 51: 1).*

> *Of the Rock who begot you,*
> *you are unmindful,*
> *And have forgotten the God*
> *who fathered you.*
> *(Deuteronomy 32: 18).*

Radical 150 (199)   谷   谷   谷

Oracle bone   Bronzeware   Traditional   Simplified

Definition: a valley, ravine, hollow

Analysis: Once again in *valley, ravine, hollow* 谷 , 俗 [59] (谷), we find ⼻ , the left portion of the character, *crossroad, to walk* ⼅ ⼦

(行 , R. 144). This pinpoints the *valley, ravine* to the area of the dividing of the four rivers from the Holy Mount. According to the pictogram of the place, *second in excellence* 𭥃 (亞 , R. [168]), there are four square spaces at the four corners of the Mount that may accommodate the four lower horns (peaks). In the radical 谷 , the 八 configuration may represent these four lower peaks or horns. A *valley, hollow* would be formed between or among the horns. The next several radicals (R. 92, 211, 86) will also display the four, lower, corner horns (peaks). The *mouth* 口 (口 , R. 30) may indicate it was at this site that Adam and Eve came to initially speak with God.

Evidently the *valley, hollow* 谷 (谷) contains water, for we find the character *to wash, bathe* 浴 60 (浴) in which an *offspring, son* 子 (子 , R. 39) is covered with *water* 水 (水 , R. 85). There, the first couple might cleanse themselves before appearing in God's presence higher on the central peak. This *cleansing, bathing* would take place in the *beautiful lake* 衍 (衍 , under R. 144), the "sea of glass," surrounding the central peak. We find that it was necessary for persons appearing in God's presence to first cleanse themselves, and their clothes. When the Hebrew slaves escaping from Egypt were to come into God's presence at Mount Sinai, they were instructed:

> Then the LORD said to Moses, "Go to the people and sanctify them today and tomorrow, and let them <u>wash their clothes</u>. And let them be ready for the third day. For on the third day the <u>LORD will come down upon Mount Sinai</u> in the sight of all the people." (Exodus 19: 10, 11).

Radical 92

                                                           牙

Seal   **Traditional**   **Simplified**

Definition: a tooth, serrated

Beginnings—Eden's Topography

Analysis: We could find no oracle bone or bronzeware rendition for either this radical or its character derivatives. Nevertheless, there is an interesting seal writing of the radical *tooth, serrated* 𒀀 ⁶¹ (牙), that could suggest the "horns" of the Holy Mount as seen in *valley* 公 (see 谷 , R. 150). Mountain peaks are often referred to as "horns" and also "teeth." In the Hebrew language, the same word, *"shen"* is used for both "crag" and "tooth."

> *Does the eagle mount up at*
>   *your command,*
> *And make its nest on high?*
> *It dwells on the rock, and resides*
> *On the <u>crag [tooth]</u> of the rock and*
>   *the stronghold.*
>   (Job 39: 27, 28).

The character for *mountain* ⛰ (山 , R. 46) shows "serration," with the jagged outline of the peaks. The four horns are at the four corners of the Holy Mountain, surrounding the "sea of glass" (see discussion of the horned altar under R. 144, p. 200). Actually, the topography of this portion of the mountain is well-illustrated by the graph 𒀭 . The figure 𒀀 in God's creating *hands* 𒀭 (臼 , R. 134) is composed of a *person* ○ (口), found between the God symbols ├ and Y (see discussion under Radicals 25 and 1). See also *earthenware pottery* 𒀭 (瓦 , R. 98) that further explains 𒀀 in 𒀀 as the first person, Adam.

Radical 211(206)

      齒   齿

Oracle bone   **Seal**   **Traditional Simplified**

Definition: teeth, to speak of, beginning

211

Analysis: *To speak of, teeth* 齒 ⁶² (齒) has a significant *Shuo Wen* Radical 38, and seal writing equivalents (齒). First, we must locate the site of the pictograms;: ∪ (凵, R. 17), as well as (亞, [R. 168]). These reveal the "sea of glass" on the Holy Mount, which is surrounded by four "horns, peaks" on the corners of the mount. (See R. 144, 150). We have already defined *teeth* (牙, R. 92) as synonymous with "horns, peaks, towers" of the Holy Mount. In the pictogram , God's fingers of His *hands* (白, R. 134) also form the "teeth" or "horns, peaks." The "horns, teeth" are quite clearly depicted in and seal radical .

The character *beginning* ⁶⁴ (齔) shows the breath ∫ emerging from among the "teeth, horns" and entering a *person* ○ (口), Adam, in God's presence (彡, R. 59). The creation of the first person, Adam is portrayed, as well as the site.

Radical 163 (34)

Oracle bone Bronzeware Traditional Simplified

Definition: a district city, a region

Analysis: In the oracle bone form of *a district city, region* ⁶⁵ (阝, 邑), we recognize the man Adam kneeling (卩, R. 26) as he worships the *Person* □ (丁), God (天, R. 113), in God's *city, region* (邑).

In the Bible we read of a city, long anticipated by the ancient faithful fathers, such as Abraham, for of him it is written:

> ...*for he waited for the <u>city</u> which has foundations, whose builder and maker is God.* (Hebrews 11: 10).

The prophet John described the city of God in great detail, we read, in part:

> *And he carried me away in the Spirit to a <u>great and high mountain</u>, and showed me the <u>great city, the holy Jerusalem</u>,.. And the <u>city is laid out as a square</u>, and its length is as great as its breadth. ...its length, breadth, and height are equal.*
> (Revelation 21: 10, 16)

At this point we should recall that the *garden* ⊞ (田, R. 102) of Eden itself is square. *Center, place, square* 𠂇 (方, R. 70), actually depicts God 𠂇. We have shown how this radical could be stretched out as ┌┐ (方), thus portraying a mountain to which the first couple 𠆢 (人, R. 9) *traveled* 𣥂 (旅). Apparently this is the Holy Mountain. It would seem to follow, therefore, that if the Garden of Eden were patterned from the heavenly original, that the "city" should be located in the center, at the top of the mountain, for this was the site to which the couple daily traveled..

> *Great is the LORD,*
>   *and greatly to be praised*
> *In the city of our God,*
> *In His holy mountain.*
> *Beautiful in elevation,*
> *The joy of the whole earth,*
> *Is Mount Zion on the sides of*
>   *the north,*
> *The city of the great King. . . .*
> *Walk about Zion,*
> *And go all around her.*
> *Count her towers;*
>   *(Psalm 48: 1, 2, 12).*

Let us next examine *the capital of a nation, a metropolis, beautiful* 都 [66] (都) which depicts not only the *city* 邑 [67] (邑), but also the glorious *tree* 木 (木 , R. 75) of life, that grew there "in the midst of the garden." Here was also the place of *speaking* 口 (口 , R. 30) with God. We read further description of the heavenly city from the prophet John:

> *And he showed me a pure river of water of life, clear as crystal, proceeding from the throne of God and of the Lamb. In the middle of its street, and on either side of the river, was the <u>tree of life</u>. . . . (Revelation 22: 1, 2)*

So we learn that from His throne in the <u>city</u>, God *looks down upon* 啚 [68] (啚) the couple as they come before Him. You will notice the *speaking Person* 入 , representing God. Beneath Him is the very site 回 , transcribed as (回 , 囬), meaning *to return to and from.* Again, observe the "squareness." Could this square area not be on the very top of the highest, central peak, the Rock, the Horn?

When this symbol 啚 is *enclosed* 囗 (囗 , R. 31) by the garden boundary, we find the character *map, diagram, plan* 圖 [69] (圖). How amazing that this character for *map, diagram, plan* is actually a pictogram of the most important feature of the Garden of Eden—the central highest tower of the Holy Mount where God 入 descended to meet with man!

So important is this character *map*, that an enlargement is made in order that every detail may be clearly seen, and today's Chinese may realize that the ancient Garden of Eden was indeed a real place!

MAP, DIAGRAM, PLAN

Radical 8 (9)

Oracle bone Bronzeware Traditional Simplified

Definition: above, (cover, top)

Analysis: This radical 亠 is difficult to interpret. There are nine *Shuo Wen* symbols for this one radical, perhaps showing its importance. There are no free-standing oracle bone or bronzeware figures, and the radical is found only in larger characters. Also, there is no one way of drawing the radical, for it takes many forms. Therefore, we will attempt to further define the location of that designated as *"above, cover, top"* from various ancient characters transcribed as carrying this radical.

It appears that 亠 is used to indicate the top-most, or above something else. In some instances it is formed from the arms and neck of 大, as in 亦 (亦), meaning *and, also, likewise;* the radical meaning *central, place, square* 方 (方, R. 70) is another example. In these instances, the figures represent God. In 立 (立), *to create, start, stand up,* however, the 大 figure represents Adam, the first human to stand up.

Another pictogram portraying God is 高 70 (高). We find the out-spread legs forms △, when the upper body 个 is eliminated. Therefore, when we find the symbol △ in 高 , 京 71 (京), meaning a *metropolis, capital, height, exalted,* we know that it represents a "dwelling place" of God "above" all else, and has taken on the shape of a mountain, or peak. Furthermore, if we invert ♈ and ♉ , we also find the Holy *Mountain* ⼭ (山 , R. 46). Could 高 , the *capital,* therefore represent the central highest peak, the "capital city" of the Garden of Eden?

Radical 189 (217)

  高 高

Oracle bone Bronzeware Traditional Simplified

Definition: high, exalted, lofty, eminent

Analysis: Now that we have found that △ represents the highest peak of the Holy Mountain (see the previous R. 8), the ancient radicals meaning *high, lofty, exalted* 侖 72 倉 73 (高) seem quite appropriate. In addition, we find the mountain 冂 itself, as well as a *mouth* ㄇ (口, R. 30) for communication of the first couple with God.

There are other features of the garden in the oracle bone rendition of *high, lofty* 喬 74 (槀) where two *trees* 林 (林, R. 75) are seen. Two special trees were found in the middle of the garden. "*The tree of life was also in the midst of the garden, and the tree of the knowledge of good and evil.*" (Genesis 2: 9). In 喬 , the trees are located on the central peak of the Holy Mountain. At this holy place, is the *seat of government* 亳 75 (亳), where the first couple worshiped God, as indicated by the uplifted *hand* ㇉ (手, R. 64). The heavenly government is based upon mercy and justice.

Radical 13 (19)

冂 冂

Oracle bone Bronzeware Traditional Simplified

Definition: a border, desert, empty, remote

Analysis: This radical has no free-standing oracle bone symbols. In fact, the transcriptions of its derived characters are poor at best! For ex-

Beginnings—Eden's Topography

ample, in *complete, entire, perfect* 𩰲, 𩰲 76 (周), the "border" is actually shaped by worshiping hands 𠂇, 𠂆 that form the Holy *Mountain* 𠂆 (厂). But between the worshiping hands is God 丫 (see R. 101), or the Great Unity 丫 (一 , R. 1). The *mouth* ᐁ (口 , R. 30) is for communion between God and the worshiper.

𠂇 𠂆 + 丫 丫 + ᐁ = 𩰲 𩰲

worshiping   Great Unity   mouth   complete, perfect
hands   (God)

The character *to put forth, issue forth* 𦫵, 𦫵 77 (冒) shows the Holy *Hill* 𠂆 (厂 , R. 27), from which two *persons* 𠆢 (人 , R. 9) emerge. Compare this with *shield* 𢆉 (干 , R. 51); 毛 (毛 , R. 82); and 𩫖 (彡 , R. 190). The latter two characters will be next discussed.

Radical 82 (112)

Oracle bone   Bronzeware   Traditional   Simplified

Definition: hair, feathers, soft-haired lamb, pure-colored sacrificial animal

Analysis: This seems to be a radical that has acquired a definition purely from its pictographic appearance, *hair, feathers* 毛 78 (毛). Note that the oracle bone figure 毛 is identical to *issue forth* 𦫵 (冒 , under R. 13), and similar to *shield* 𢆉 (干 , R. 51) and *excellent, chosen one* 𩫖 (彡 , R. 190). Why are there two *persons* 𠆢 on the Holy Mount 𠂆 ? The bronzeware form 𨳍 79 (毛) surely looks like a feather, but the black dot ● on 𨳍 suggests holiness, while the 𢆉 configuration is also consistent

The Beginning of Chinese Characters

with "God" 丫 as seen in *to travel* 㫃 (旅 , under R. 70), and in *venerable, old* 𠈹 (老 , R. 125). We will discuss the figure 𡴁 further under this radical.

Radical 190 (219)

Oracle bone Bronzeware Traditional Simplified

Definition: hair, shaggy

Analysis: We could find no free-standing oracle bone or bronzeware pictograms for this radical, but there is a derived character, such as *eminent, excellent, chosen one* 㲎 ⁸⁰ (髦) that is similar to *issue forth* 冃 (冒 , under R. 13). The 冂 appears to be the same as 人 (see under R. 82).

Hair on the head 𢒰 ⁸¹ (髮) is actually the glorious God, indicated by the *sun* ☉ (日 , R. 72) and the ╎╎╎ is "God's presence (彡 , R. 59).

The character *whiskers, beard* 𩈲 ⁸² (髯), we find, is actually portraying features of the Holy Mountain. The *"whiskers"* are depicting the four rivers 𠘧 flowing from the "sea of glass." (See R. 47). If 𢒰 and 𩈲 are pictograms of God, so is the character meaning *wait, expect, whiskers* 𩇨 ⁸³ (鬚). Again, the *river* 巛 (川 , R. 47) is seen flowing from a basin-like depression ∪ , evidently a depiction of the lake on the Holy Mountain. (See R. 17 for the answer to who or what is *awaited or expected*).

Radical 125

  老

Oracle bone Bronzeware Traditional Simplified

Definition: venerable, aged, old-established, (Godhead)

Analysis: There are as many representations of this radical as there are definitions: *venerable, aged, long-established, term of respect* 丙, 犬, 耂, 耂 [84] (老). Is the "old man" depicted in 丙 leaning on a cane? It would seem that *perfect* | (十, R. 24) pictures rather a *man* 人 (人 , R. 9) as interpreted in the corresponding bronzeware symbol 耂 [85] (老), whom God is creating. God is representing by ◊ (丶 , R. 3); 爪 (爪 , R. 87); 丫 (甫 , under R. 101); and 耂 (一, R. 1 and 59) in the var!ous portrayals of the *venerable Person*. So we have established that the *venerable* Person is God, portrayed as the Holy Mount. The Bible has a vivid record of the picture of God,

> "I watched till thrones were put in place,
> And the <u>Ancient of Days</u> was seated;
> His garment was white as snow,
> And the hair of His head was
>   like pure wool.
> His throne was a fiery flame,
> Its wheels a burning fire;
> A fiery stream issued
> And came forth before Him."
>   Daniel 7: 9,10

To further confirm this claim, let us examine *filial, to honor one's parents* 耂, 耂 [86] (孝). In this character we recognize *two* 丨丨 *offspring* 子 (子 , R. 39), the first "offspring" of God, Adam and his wife. The *Person* 人 (人 , R. 9) in 耂 forms the Holy Mount. But in 耂 we find the Godhead: the *Father* 父 (父 , R. 88); a second *Noble* 大 (大 , R. 37) Person with arms upraised; and ◊ (丶 , R. 3) representing the third Person. This combination of 耂 takes the place of 丙, also revealing the three Persons of the Godhead.

The Beginning of Chinese Characters

The character *old age, complete* ⁸⁷ (考) shows the *breath* 丁 (丂) of life coming from the Godhead on the Holy Mount whose creative *hand* (爪, R. 87) is outstretched.

Radical 168

Oracle bone Bronzeware Traditional Simplified

Definition: Long (in space or time), old, increase, respect for age

Analysis: This radical is similar to Radicals 125 and 190, and also reveals the Godhead and the Holy Mount. *Excelling, old, long (in space or time)* ⁸⁸ (長) defines the Godhead who are immortal. The symbol identifies God. The depiction is nearly identical to (老, R. 125), both showing the creation of man (十, R. 24). This character in the bronzeware (長) portrays the Holy Mount (厂, R. 27) as well as the Godhead .

Radical 86 (80, 83)

Oracle bone Bronzeware Traditional Simplified

Definition: fire, flame

Analysis: *Fire* ⁸⁹ (火) takes many forms in the oracle bone writing. This is such an important radical, and used in so many characters that it has been difficult to know where to place it chronologically.

The "fire" and "mountain" graphs are quite similar, and with good rea-

Beginnings—Eden's Topography

son, as we have learned in Section III, R. 46. We also found in Section II that the first man and woman, *"made in God's image"* (Genesis 1:26), had a fiery appearance 🔥 (赤, R. 155). In fact, the bronzeware graph for *fire* 🔥 ₉₀ actually reveals a symbol of the first man of *clay* 👤 (土) with flames coming from him (see R. 32)!

Both the Chinese and Hebrew sacrificial ceremonies involved burning the animals after they had been killed. The graph *Lamb* 🔥 ⁹¹ (羔) shows a *lamb, sheep* 🐑 (羊) representing Jesus, being burned in the *fire* 🔥 (火), or as a sacrifice on the *mountain* ⛰ (山) of Calvary. Recall that the characters for *fire* and *mountain* are identical in the oracle bone (R. 86 and R. 46).

But now let us examine carefully this most beautiful and meaningful graph for *Lamb* 🔥 (羔). Do you see the figure 大, meaning *Tian, Heaven, God* 大 (天, R. [90]) with arms upraised—as the arms of Jesus were upraised on the cross? Furthermore, do you recognize the four "horns" ⛰ at the corners of the Holy Mountain? These form the horned altar on which the Lamb of God was sacrificed. (See *horn* 角 [角], R. 148, p. 196, and also Figure 1). The symbol of *Tian, Heaven, God* 大 (天) forms the central tower of the mountain. Jesus Christ is not only the *Horn* 角 (角, R. 148) of Salvation; but also the *Rock* 石 (石, R. 112), the chief Corner Stone; our *Shield* 干 (干, R. 51); our *Deliverer* 匚 (匚); our *Strength* 力 (力, R. 19); and our high *Tower* 丨 (一, R. 1), synonymous with the *Great Unity*, the Godhead!

In order for us to fully appreciate this magnificent *Lamb* character, we will enlarge it.

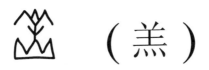

Now read these verses:

> *God is the LORD,*
> *And He has given us light;*
> *Bind the sacrifice with cords to*
> *the horns of the altar .*
> *(Psalm 118: 27).*

> *And the city [the New Jerusalem] had no need of the sun or of the moon to shine in it, for the glory of God illuminated it, and the <u>Lamb is its light</u>. (Revelation 21: 23).*

After exploring the Holy Mountain in this Section, one can appreciate how the Chinese repeatedly and painstakingly emphasized this central feature of the Garden of Eden. The Bible supplies topographical hints as to the shape and notable details of the Holy Mount (review "Harel," p. 198, Figure 1). These are also miraculously contained in many pictographic ancient Chinese characters. The relationship of the Mountain and the Godhead —even Their Personification as the Holy Mount, and Jesus Christ as the central Tower, Rock, Horn, etc. —— have all been cleverly portrayed, so that one is not left in doubt as to the Chinese esteem and awe of this site.

Of one thing we must be certain. The early Chinese were <u>not</u> pagans, but followers of the true God, "Tian," [Heaven], or "Shangdi" [God], as they called Him. Shangdi [Tian] was likewise interested in the Chinese! Recorded in their ancient classical writings, we find this statement:

The great Tian [Heaven] gave this Middle Kingdom [ancient China] with it people and territories to the former kings.[92]

On the other hand, Eden's Holy Mount, as we have found it an earthly miniature of the heavenly Mount Zion, has been counterfeited world-wide by the pagans. The first counterfeit, it would seem, was likely the Tower of Babel— which would surely account for God's great displeasure, his halting of the construction of this edifice by the confusion of language, and the scattering of the rebellious ones far and wide.

According to Faber, quoted at the first of this section, "The pyramid with seven stages presents the complete similitude of the sacred Babylonian tower, which was dedicated to the great father Belus [Bel]. . . .Babel became the beginning, at once of the meditated empire, and of the determined apostasy, of Nimrod. <u>That tower in short was the first imitative pyramid.</u> . . . I think there can be little doubt, that the structure begun by Nimrod was the identical pyramid, which Herodotus [5th century B.C. historian] describes as the temple of Belus. . . .

"When Babylon regained its pristine importance, Nebuchadnezzar. . .I think . . .completed what Nimrod left unfinished, and consequently that the temple of Belus was the original tower now finished according to the design of its first founder. Herodotus informs us, that the Babylonic temple of Belus was a vast square building: that in the midst of this sacred enclosure rose a massy tower of the depth and height of a single stadium: the tower itself was composed of seven towers. . . . successively diminishing in size from the bottom to the top. The ascent, he says, wound round it on the outside, thus imitating the circuitous ascent of a mountain."[93]

Several additional names are appended to this tower: "Tower of Jupiter Belus," "Temple of the Seven Lights of the Earth," the "Temple of Tongues," and the "Ziggurat of Borsippa." Furthermore, there is a "Borsippa Inscription," written by Nebuchadnezzar, that reads:

"A former king built it (they reckon forty-two ages), but he did not complete its head. <u>Since a remote time, people had abandoned</u>

it, without order expressing their words. Since that time the earthquake and the thunder had dispersed its sun-dried clay; the bricks of the casing had been split, and the earth of the interior had been scattered in heaps. Merodach, the great lord, excited my mind to repair this building. I did not change the site, nor did I take away the foundation stone. As it had been in former times so I founded, I made it; as it had been in ancient days so I exalted its summit."[94]

Further description of the great Babylonian tower was suggested by historian Will Durant in his *The Story of Civilization:* "Approaching the city the traveler saw first—at the crown of a very mountain of masonry—an immense and lofty *ziggurat,* rising in seven stages of gleaming enamel to a height of 650 feet. . . .This structure, taller than the pyramids of Egypt, and surpassing in height all but the latest of modern buildings, was probably the 'Tower of Babel.'"[95]

Durant gives this additional description: "The great *ziggurat* at Borsippa was called 'the Stages of the Seven Spheres'; each story was dedicated to one of the seven planets known to Babylonia, and bore a symbolic color. The lowest was black, as the color of Saturn; the next above it was white, as the color of Venus; the next was purple, for Jupiter; the fourth blue, for Mercury; the fifth scarlet, for Mars; the sixth silver, for the moon; the seventh gold, for the sun. These spheres and stars, beginning at the top, designated the days of the week."[96] (Figure 2).

We find worldwide today that the days of the week, in various languages, have followed this very same scheme of designation. We can also know that from the time of Babylon, the pagans worshiped the sun and dedicated Sunday, the first day, to its worship. Is it not possible that the Tower of Babel [pyramid of Belus, Ziggurat of Borsippa] was a defrauded imitation of the most holy middle tower of the original Holy Mount of Eden where original face-to-face worship of God took place? Could the Babel architects have ap-

Figure 1

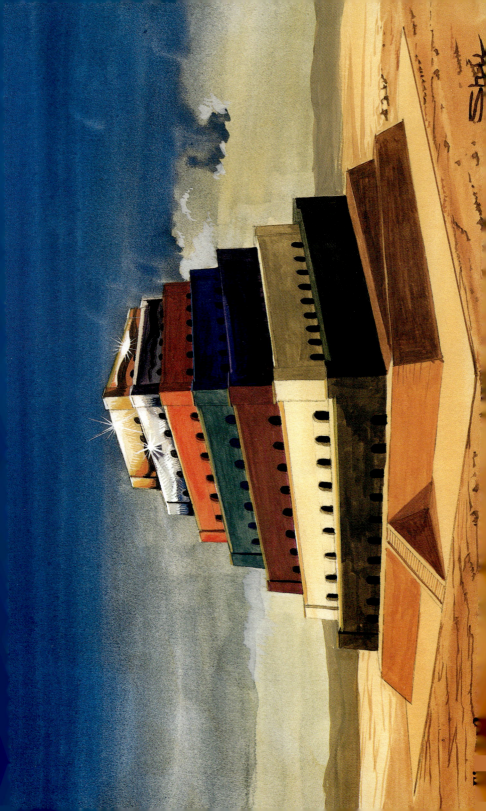

Figure 3

Figure 5

Figure 6

Figure 7

pended their false religious concepts to their own holy mountain?

> *For since the creation of the world His invisible attributes are clearly seen, being understood by the things that are made, even His eternal power and Godhead, so that they are without excuse, because, <u>although they knew God, they did not glorify Him as God</u>, nor were thankful, but became futile in their thoughts, and their foolish hearts were darkened.*
> *(Romans 1: 20, 21).*

Lucifer himself had pompously bragged:

> *"I will ascend into heaven,*
> *I will exalt my throne above*
> *the stars of God;*
> *<u>I will also sit on the mount</u>*
> *<u>of the congregation</u>*
> *On the farthest sides of the*
> *north;*
> *I will ascend above the heights*
> *of the clouds,*
> *I will be like the Most High."*
> *(Isaiah 14: 13, 14).*

And so we find Satan-inspired mythical mountains of false worship spreading far and wide throughout the earth. Faber states further, "The tradition of the Hindoos [Hindus] seems to be more embodied and better connected than that of any other nation. Perhaps also it may serve as a kind of key to the right understanding of parallel legends. . . . <u>In the fabled [Mount] Meru of Hindoo theology may be recognized the Mosaical garden of Eden.</u>. . .It is said to be of four different colours towards the four cardinal points [yellow, red, white, and brown]. Some imagine <u>its form to be that of a square pyramid.</u> . . .
"<u>The Hindoos believe, that the four rivers of Meru spring from the roots of</u>

<u>Jambu, a tree of most extravagant size, which is thought to convey knowledge</u>. ...Now it is the universal persuasion of the Hindoos, that [Meru] is the origin of the Ganges. . . .They suppose, that a river first flows round the city of Brahma; that next it discharges itself into the lake Mansarovara; and that thence it issues through the rocky heads of four animals [cow, horse, elephant, and lion], constituting four streams which run to the four quarters of the globe.(Figure 3). The Hindoos describe their holy mountain Meru as terminating in three peaks [a profile view from any one of its four sides]. [97]

Aside from the mythical replicas of Eden's original Holy Mount are artifices still standing today in various parts of the world. The Holy Mount of Eden's central "high tower," God's "dwelling place," the city sought by Abraham *"which has foundations, whose builder and maker is God" (Hebrews 11: 10)*, and the place of God's throne— is mimicked by many "stepped" pyramids, such as Egypt's most ancient pyramid of Djoser [Zoser], made of small stone blocks (Figure 4)[98] ; and El Tajin in Venezula (Figure 5). These would possibly most closely resemble the Tower of Babel.

Perhaps the best replica of the entire Holy Mount is the Golden Mount in Bangkok Thailand, a large artificial, cement-covered hill on which a large, central, golden pagoda is surrounded on four corners by lower golden pagodas (Figure 6). The main temple complex at Angkor Wat in Cambodia demonstrates the same architectural features[99] (Figures 7) with the four lower towers at the lower corners surrounding a central high, stepped tower.

While the Chinese radicals portray concepts in keeping with Biblical truth, the pagan ideas have wandered into mystical veins and false worship of the cosmos, even though the early pagans possessed a common knowledge of a great original Eden model. In this Section under consideration, we have found that the spurious may look like the true.

Why cannot we find any of these counterfeited pyramids, or any traces of their former existence in the land of ancient China? This may suggest another proof that the clear knowledge of God has kept the ancient Chinese from falling into Babylonian superstitions. The pagodas widely seen in China today were imported by Buddhists from India at a much later date.

Could we but actually see what Adam and Eve beheld so many years ago in the Garden of Eden—that sacred Holy Mount with its resplendent beauty! We, like Abraham of old, can not only seek, but one day actually become acquainted first hand, with the great celestial original and its exquisite loveliness! However many events will intervene before we can actually behold God's glorious dwelling place.

Of one thing we may be certain. The prophet John in the Revelation has given us insight into the appearance of the holy New Jerusalem which one day will descend from heaven. What a gorgeous jewel-bedecked satellite, the Holy City that Abraham sought, will be! (Figure 8).

> *"And I saw a new heaven and a new earth, for the first heaven and the first earth had passed away. Also there was no more sea. Then I, John, saw the holy city, New Jerusalem, coming down out of heaven from God, prepared as a bride adorned for her husband. . . . Now the wall of the city had twelve foundations. . . . And the city is laid out as a square. . . . Its length, breadth, and height are equal. . . . And the foundations of the wall of the city were adorned with all kinds of precious stones: the first foundation was jasper, the second sapphire, the third chalcedony, the fourth emerald, the fifth sardonyx, the sixth sardius, the seventh chrysolite, the eighth beryl, the ninth topaz, the tenth chrysoprase, the eleventh jacinth, and the twelfth amethyst. And the twelve gates were twelve pearls. And the street of the city was pure gold, like transparent glass.*
>   *(Revelation 21: 2, 14, 16, 19-21).*
>
> *And the city had no need of the sun or of the moon to shine in it, for the glory of God illuminated it, and the Lamb is its light.*

And the nations of those who are saved shall walk in its light, and the kings of the earth bring their glory and honor into it. Its gates shall not be shut at all by day (there shall be no night there)...

Blessed are those who do His commandments, that they may have the right to the tree of life, and may enter through the gates into the city.   (Revelation 21: 23-25; 22: 14).

---

[1] George Stanley Faber, *The Origin of Pagan Idolatry* (London: R. & C. Rivingtons, 1816), Vol. I, p. vii.

[2] CKWP, no. 8.12.

[3] HPC, no. 8.24

[4] Ibid., no. 7.4.

[5] HPC, no. 7.4.

[6] MWC, no. 629.

[7] Ibid., no. 9.8.

[8] Ibid., no. 11.1.

[9] HPC, no, 11.1.

[10] CKWP, no. 11.10.

[11] Ibid., no. 11.3

[12] CKWP, no. 11.9.

[13] HPC, no. 11.5.

[14] MWC, p. 1019.

[15] CKWP, no. 11.10.
[16] Ibid., no. 7.27.
[17] HPC, no. 4.5
[18] CKWP, no. 11.10.
[19] ZHL, pp. 29, 96.
[20] HPC, no. 3.1.
[21] CKWP, no. 4.24.
[22] HPC, no. 4.25.
[23] MWC, p. 1336, CKWP, No. 13.6.
[24] CKWP, no. 1.2.
[25] HPC, no. 1.3.
[26] MWC, p. 1167.
[27] HPC, no. 14.16.
[28] Ibid., p. 849.
[29] MWC, p. 517
[30] CKWP, no, 2.23.
[31] HPC, no. 2.30
[32] MWC, p. 145
[33] HPC 11.3.
[34] MWC, p. 58.
[35] Chung-kuo k'e hsueh-yuan k'ao-ku yen-chiu-so, *Chia Ku Wen-Pien* (Peking: K'ao-ku-hsueh chuan-k'an yi-chung ti-shih-ssu hao, 1965), No. 2.19. [Hereafter abbreviated CKWP].
[36] Op. Cit., HPC, no. 2.15.
[37] CKWP, no. 8.15.
[38] Op. cit., ZS, p. 122.
[39] CKWP, no. 8.27.
[40] MWC, p. 507.
[41] ZSL, p. 31.

42 HPC, no. 3.9.
43 LCC, Sn. 17, p. 15.
44 CKWP, nO. 2.15.
45 Ibid., no. 2.18.
46 HPC, no. 2.19.
47 CKWP, no. 2.17.
48 Ibid., no. 14.5.
49 Ibid., no. 11.8.
50 MWC, p. 21.
51 Ibid. p. 23.
52 HPC, no. 2.27.
53 Ibid., no. 8.10.
54 MWC, p. 25.
55 CKWP, no. 2.19.
56 CKWP, no. 6.7, 6.8.
57 Ibid., no. 3.5.
58 Ibid. no. 3.5.
59 Ibid., no. 11.11, 2.27.
60 MWC, p. 1140.
61 LCC, Sn. 3, p. 31.
62 MWC, p. 765.
63 LCC, Sn. 5, p. 4.
64 MWC, p. 767.
65 CKWP, no. 6.11.
66 HPC, no. 6.23.
67 Ibid., no. 6.22.
68 Ibid., no. 5.36.
69 Ibid., no. 6.15.
70 Ibid., 5.23.

[71] Ibid., no. 5.23.
[72] Ibid., no. 5.20.
[73] HPC, no. 5.33.
[74] CKWP, no. 6.1
[75] Ibid., no. 5.21.
[76] Ibid., no. 2.9.
[77] MWC, p. 1102.
[78] Ibid. p. 1103.
[79] HPC, no. 8.19.
[80] MWC, p. 1104.
[81] Ibid., p. 398.
[82] Ibid., p. 447.
[83] Ibid., p. 397.
[84] Ibid., no. 8.10.
[85] HPC, no. 8.14.
[86] Ibid, no. 8.19.
[87] Ibid., no. 8.17.
[88] MWC, p. 404.
[89] CKWP no. 10.7-10.9; HCKWP no. 10.10-10.12.
[90] Hung Pei Chiang, Chih Ku Lu Chuan Wen (Taipei: Lo Pien Publ. Co., 1974), vol. ii, p. 1302. [Hereafter abbreviated HPC vol. II]
[91] Ibid., no. 4.13.
[92] James Legge, *The Chinese Classics*, (Taipei: SMC Publishing, Inc. 1983), Vol. III, *The Shu Jing*, Pt. V, Bk. XI, Para. 6, p. 418ve
[93] Op. cit. George Stanley Faber, Vol. III, pp. 239, 240.
[94] Smith, William, *Dictionary of the Bible* (Hartford: J.B Burr & Co., 1868), p. 713
[95] Will Durant, *The Story of Civilization: Our Oriental Heritage, Babylonia* (New York: Simon and Schuster, 1941), p. 225.

[96] Ibid., p. 255.

[97] Op. cit. George Stanley Faber, Vol. I, pp. 314-317.

[98] *The Horizon Book of Lost Worlds* (New York: American Heritage Publ. Co., 1962), p. 46.

[99] Malcolm MacDonald, *Angkor* (London: Jonathan Cape, 30 Bedford Square, 1958).

Notes

Notes

Appendix I

"My Holy Hill"

Ethel R. Nelson

The Bible is replete with references to "My Holy Hill." The question naturally arises, where is this hill? Why is is so often mentioned in the Bible, especially the Psalms? Psalm 99: 9 states: *"Exalt the LORD our God, And worship at His holy hill; For the LORD our God is holy."* This hill is a place of worship. Looking at the first three verses of the same Psalm, we read:

> *The LORD reigns;*
> *Let the peoples tremble!*
> *He dwells between the cherubim;*
> *Let the earth be moved!*
> *The LORD is great in <u>Zion,</u>*
> *And He is high above all the peoples.*
> *Let them praise Your great and awesome name—*
> *He is holy.. . .*
> *Exalt the LORD our God,*
> *And worship at His footstool;*
> *For He is holy.*
>   *(Psalm 99: 1-3, 5).*

In these verses, we find that the Holy Hill is called Zion, from which place God reigns, while the people worship at "His footstool." *"Thus says the LORD: "Heaven is My throne, And the earth is My footstool." (Isaiah 66: 1`); "Let us go into His tabernacle; Let us worship at His footstool" (Psalm 132: 7).*

Furthermore, Psalm 132: 13 declares:

For the LORD has chosen <u>Zion;</u>
He has desired it for His habitation:
<u>"This is My resting place forever;</u>
Here I will dwell, for I have desired it."

We will shortly learn of Mount Zion's interesting history. But now let us investigate the various "holy hills" in the Bible. It was the presence of God ["theophany"] on a mountain that made it holy. Perhaps the first to be considered, therefore, might be Mount Ararat where Noah's ark rested after the worldwide flood. It was here that Noah built an altar and offered one of every clean beast and fowl which had been preserved in the ark. (Genesis 8: 20). On Ararat God covenanted with Noah that there would never again be a flood to destroy the earth. The token of the covenant was a rainbow. God promised: *"I set My rainbow in the cloud, and it shall be for a sign of the covenant between Me and the earth... the waters shall never again become a flood to destroy all flesh." (Genesis 9: 13, 15).*

Doubtless the most spectacular mountain in the Old Testament was Mount Sinai (Horeb). Several dramatic scenes took place under its shadow, or on its top. The LORD Himself appeared to Moses in a burning bush at *"Horeb, the mountain of God" (Exodus 3: 1)*, identifying Himself: *"And God said to Moses, 'I AM WHO I AM,'" (Exodus 3: 14)*, and instructed Moses to lead the Israelites out of Egypt. God also said, *"When you have brought the people out of Egypt, <u>you shall serve God on this mountain.</u>" (Exodus 3: 13)*, thus looking forward to the future giving of the Ten Commandments on this site.

When the Israelites were in the wilderness and had run out of water,

Appendix I—My Holy Hill

God instructed Moses, *"Behold, I will stand before you there on the rock in Horeb; and you shall strike the rock, and water will come out of it, that the people may drink." (Exodus 17: 6)*. This was a prophecy of the death of Jesus, the mighty "Rock," with His wounded side from which flowed water and blood (John 19:34). Jesus, the "water of life" would bring salvation to His people.

After the Israelites had encamped at the base of Mt. Sinai, God gave them specific instructions.

> *Then the LORD said to Moses,*
> *"Go to the people and sanctify them today and tomorrow, and let them wash their clothes. And let them be ready for the third day. For on the third day the LORD will come down upon Mount Sinai in the sight of all the people. You shall set bounds for the people all around, saying, 'Take heed to yourselves that you do not go up to the mountain or touch its base. Whoever touches the mountain shall surely be put to death.'" (Exodus 19: 10-13)*.

As the LORD came down upon the mountain and pronounced the Ten Commandments, Mount Sinai was covered with fire and smoke. There were thunderings, lightning, and the sound of the trumpet. The whole mountain quaked greatly. The people trembled with fear and awe. The LORD invited Moses, Aaron, Nadab and Abihu, and seventy of the elders of Israel to come up on to the mountain and worship from afar.

> *"And they saw the God of Israel,. And there was <u>under His feet as it were a paved work of sapphire stone, and it was like the very heavens in its clarity.</u> . . .Then the LORD said to Moses, 'Come up to Me on the mountain and be there; and I will give you tablets of stone, and the law and commandments which I have written, that you may teach them.'": (Exodus 24: 9, 10, 12)*.

Does not this area under God's feet [His footstool], *"a paved work of sapphire stone"* . . . *"like the very heavens in its clarity"* sound like the "Sea of Glass," God's "footstool? [See Radicals (168), 144, pp. 199-203].

Moses alone went up higher on the mountain, which appeared to be on fire with the glory of the LORD.

> *Then the LORD said to Moses, "Come up to Me on the mountain and be there; and I will give you tablets of stone, and the law and commandments which I have written, that you may teach them." (Exodus 24: 12).*

Moses communed there with God for 40 days and nights. It was on Sinai that God wrote the Ten Commandments with His own finger on stone, thus confirming the perpetuiity of His law. Fire was a manifestation of the presence of God on Sinai, thus making the mountain a "Holy Hill."

Another Holy Hill recurs again and again in the Old Testament—Mount Moriah. It was here that God tested Abraham, the "father of the faithful," asking him to sacrifice his only beloved son, Isaac. As Abraham sorrowfully lifted the knife to slay his son, the Angel of the LORD [the LORD Himself] commanded him to stop, saying *"Now I know that you fear God, since you have not withheld your son, your only son, from Me." (Genesis 22: 12).* And there was a ram caught in a thicket by its horns. Abraham offered it instead of his son. The sheep was a symbol of the coming "Lamb of God" [Jesus Christ] who would substitute His own life for all mankind.

> *"For God so loved the world that He gave His only begotten Son, that whoever believes in Him should not perish but have everlasting life." (John 3: 16).*

This very site on Mount Moriah many years later became the threshing floor of Ornan, the Jebusite. God commanded King David to erect an altar there.

> *So David gave Ornan six hundred shekels of gold by weight for the place. And David built there an altar to the LORD, and offered burnt offerings and peace offerings, and called on the LORD; and He answered him from heaven by fire on the altar of burnt offering. (1 Chronicles 21: 25, 26).*

A few years later a still more important event took place at this very site on Mount Moriah. Solomon, King David's son, built there a beautiful temple for God

> Now Solomon began to build the house of the LORD at Jerusalem on Mount Moriah, where the LORD had appeared to his father David, at the place that David had prepared on the threshing floor of Ornan the Jebusite. (2 Chronicles 3: 1).

Mount Moriah therefore became Mount Zion, and Jerusalem, its capital city. The temple was built on the same scheme as the sanctuary in the Wilderness [see Appendix II, "Significance of the Sanctuary"], with two apartments. The Most Holy Place contained the golden ark. *"There was nothing in the ark except the two tablets [upon which were written with God's own finger the Ten Commandments] which Moses put there at Horeb."* (2 Chronicles 5: 10). *"For the cherubim [of gold] spread their wings over the place of the ark, and the cherubim overshadowed the ark"* (2 Chronicles 5: 8). As the temple was dedicated with great ceremony and grandeur, the LORD Himself descended and *"the house of the LORD was filled with a cloud, so that the priests could not continue ministering because of the cloud; for the glory of the LORD filled the house of God."* (2 Chronicles 5: 13, 14).

The earthly Zion with its city, Jerusalem, became a "type" [prophetic symbol] of the heavenly dwelling place of God, to be inhabited in the future by God's faithful people from the earth:

> *"Your eyes will see the King in His beauty;*
> *They will see the land that is very far off. . . .*
> *Look upon Zion, the city of our appointed feasts;*
> *Your eyes will see Jerusalem, a quiet habitation,*
> *A tabernacle that will not be taken down;*
> *Not one of its stakes will ever be removed,*
> *Nor will any of its cords be broken.*
> *But there the majestic LORD will be for us*

> *A place of broad rivers and streams,*
> *In which no galley with oars will sail,*
> *Nor majestic ships pass by*
> *(For the LORD is our Judge,*
> *The LORD is our lawgiver,*
> *The LORD is our King;*
> *He will save us)." (Isaiah 33: 17, 20-22)*

It will be the Savior, Christ Jesus, the LORD, who has been our Judge, Advocate, and King, and will be so forever in the heavenly courts.

The New Testament also is not lacking in Holy Hills, When Jesus walked the earth as a Man, he preached from the "Mount of Blessing."

> *And seeing the multitudes, He went up on a mountain, and when He was seated His disciples came to Him. Then He opened His mouth and taught them, saying:*
> *"Blessed are the poor in spirit,*
> *For theirs is the kingdom of heaven.*
> *Blessed are those who mourn,*
> *For they shall be comforted.*
> *Blessed are the meek,*
> *For they shall inherit the earth.*
> *Blessed are those who hunger and thirst*
> *for righteousness,*
> *For they shall be filled.*
> *Blessed are the merciful,*
> *For they shall obtain mercy.*
> *Blessed are the pure in heart,*
> *For they shall see God.*
> *Blessed are the peacemakers,*
> *For they shall be called sons of God.*
> *Blessed are those who are persecuted*
> *for righteousness' sake,*
> *For theirs is the kingdom of heaven.*
> *(Matthew 5: 1-10).*

Appendix I—My Holy Hill

Jesus was also transfigured on a Mount. Jesus took three of His disciples, Peter, James, and John "*up on a high mountain by themselves, and was transfigured before them. His face shone like the sun, and His clothes became as white as the light. And behold, Moses and Elijah appeared to them, talking with Him. . . .behold, a bright cloud overshadowed them; and suddenly a voice came out of the cloud, saying, 'This is My beloved Son, in whom I am well pleased. Hear Him!" (Matthew 17: 1-3, 5)*.

What a privilege for these three disciples to witness this scene of splendor, and to hear God the Father's voice commending His Son, and personally advising the disciples to listen to the words of Jesus!

A final Holy Hill is the Mount of Olives from which Jesus ascended into heaven, accompanied by a cloud of angels.

> *While they watched, He was taken up, and a cloud received out of their sight. And while they looked steadfastly toward heaven as He went up, behold two men stood by them in white apparel [angels], who also said, "Men of Galilee, why do you stand gazing up into heaven? This same Jesus, who was taken up from you into heaven, will so come in like manner as you saw Him go into heaven." Then they returned to Jerusalem from the Mount called Olivet, which is near Jerusalem, a Sabbath day's journey. (Acts 1: 9-12)*.

And so it was that Jesus was taken up into heaven from a Holy Hill, the Mount of Olives. The prophet John, looking into the future wrote:

> *"And I saw a new heaven and a new earth, for the first heaven and the first earth had passed away. Also there was no more sea. Then I, John, saw the holy city, New Jerusalem, coming down out of heaven from God, prepared as a baride adorned for her husband And I heard a loud voice from heaven saying, 'Behold the tabernacle of God is with men, and He will dwell with them, and they shall be His people, and God Himself will*

be with them and be their God." (Revelation 21: 1-3).

Regarding the "new earth" which God will prepare, the prophet Isaiah wrote over 2,000 years ago, quoting the Lord God:

> *"For behold, I create new*
> *heavens and a new earth;*
> *And the former shall not be*
> *remembered or come to mind....*
> *They shall build houses*
> *and inhabit them;*
> *They shall plant vineyards*
> *and eat their fruit.*
> *They shall not build*
> *and another inhabit;*
> *They shall not plant and*
> *another eat;*
> *For as the days of a tree,*
> *so shall be the days of My people,*
> *And My elect shall long enjoy*
> *the work of their hands. . . .*
> *They shall not hurt nor destroy*
> <u>*in all My holy mountain,*</u>*"*
> *Says the LORD.*
> *(Isaiah 65: 17, 21,22,25).*

Then, in the earth made new, all nations shall come to worship God, their Creator and Friend.

> *"For as the new heavens*
> *and the new earth*
> *Which I will make shall remain*
> *before Me," says the LORD,*
> *"So shall your descendants*
> *and your name remain*
> *And it shall come to pass*

> *That from one New Moon to another,*
> *And from one Sabbath to another,*
> *All flesh shall come to worship*
> *before Me," says the LORD*
> *(Isaiah 66: 22, 23).*

Make a joyful shout to the LORD,
   all the earth!
Serve the LORD with gladness;
Come before His presence with singing.
Know that the LORD, he is God;
It is He who has made us,
   and not we ourselves;
We are His people and the sheep
   of His pasture.
Enter into His gates with thanksgiving,
And into His courts with praise.
Be thankful to Him, and bless His name.
For the Lord is good;
His mercy is everlasting,
And His truth endures to all generations.
                    (Psalm 100).

The Beginning of Chinese Characters

Appendix II

Significance of the Sanctuary

Ethel R. Nelson

"*In the beginning God created the heavens and the earth.*"*(Genesis 1: 1)*. It took God just six literal days to complete His wonderful creative work. On the sixth day of that first week, *"God created man in His own image; in the image of God He created him; male and female He created them." (Genesis 1: 27)*. God gave the world and everything in it as a gift to His new creatures, man and woman. It was gladsome occasion *"When the morning stars [angels] sang together, and all the sons of God [inhabitants of other worlds] shouted for joy." (Job 38: 7)*.

"*Thus the heavens and the earth, and all the host of them, were finished. And on the seventh day God ended His work which He had done, and He rested on the seventh day from all His work which He had done. Then God blessed the seventh day and sanctified it, because in it He rested from all His work which God had created and made." (Genesis 2: 1-3)*. Thus man celebrated with God at the end of the wonderful creation week, and enjoyed open communion with his Maker, the God of the universe.

However, this intimate communion was broken because of the intrusion of disobedience and sin that resulted in man's spiritual fall. Sin not only resulted in man's loss of his original lordship over the earth, but also separated him from his Creator. Man's very existence would have come to an end had not a wonderful plan of salvation for man been immediately instituted. Jesus Christ, *"the Lamb slain from the foundation of the world," (Revelation 13: 8),* stepped forward and offered to die in man's stead. How all heaven must have grieved over the plight of man. But it was God's purpose to restore man to his original position by this plan of redemption now introduced.

But how could God reveal to man His great plan for man's salvation and renew the broken communion? In turn, how could man learn of and understand God's plan for saving him from death because of his disobedience? The Bible points man to the sanctuary [tabernacle].

The word "sanctuary" occurs 144 times in the Old and New Testaments of the Bible. This word means "a dwelling place for the Most High God." It is a sacred place where God could dwell among men, where His presence could be manifested [theophany]. There is no record in the Bible of a sanctuary for the first twenty-five centuries, but instead there are repeated instances of God's appearing to righteous men in the form of "the Angel of the Lord" [theophany, the presence of Jesus Christ, Himself]. The first mention of an actual sanctuary in the Bible is in the book of Exodus.

After God's chosen leader, Moses, led over 2,000,000 Israelites out of Egyptian slavery into the Sinai wilderness, the LORD commanded Moses: *"And let them make Me a sanctuary, that I may dwell among them." (Exodus 25: 8).* Moses was given specific instructions by God, whom he visited on Mount Sinai, as to every particular in the building of a portable sanctuary: size, shape, materials and use. God said, *"And see to it that you make them according to the <u>pattern</u> which was shown you on the mountain." (Exodua 25: 40).*

Just what was the "pattern" that God specified, and what was its significance? In the New Testament book of Hebrews, we read,

Appendix II—Significance of the Sanctuary

"We have such a High Priest [Jesus Christ], who is seated at the right hand of the throne of the Majesty in the heavens, a Minister of the sanctuary and of the <u>true tabernacle which the Lord erected, and not man</u>." (Hebrews 8: 1,2).

Today, our High Priest, Jesus Christ, is ministering in the heavenly original tabernacle, built by God, Himself.

"For Christ has not entered the <u>holy places made with hands, which are copies of the true</u>, but into heaven itself, now to appear in the presence of God for us." (Hebrews 9: 24).

So we learn that the sanctuary which Moses was instructed to build was patterned after the great original in heaven. The tabernacle itself consisted of two apartments: the Most Holy Place, whose length, width and height were equal, making it cubical; and the Holy Place, whose dimensions were the same except for a doubled length. A courtyard surrounding the sanctuary was also based upon two squares. These structures were surrounded at a distance by the entire Israelite encampment, perfectly forming yet a greater square. So we find that in the very center of the encampment was the Most Holy Place where God's glorious presence was manifested (see drawing).

There were multiple purposes for the sanctuary:
- God's dwelling place in the midst to give counsel, encouragement, and the assurance of His constant leadership.
- For an object lesson
- To visually demonstrate the Plan of Salvation
- To symbolize the many attributes of Jesus Christ, their ultimate Savior
- To provide a visual demonstration of the results of sin.
- To assure repentant mankind that through the blood of Jesus, sins could ultimately be forgiven.

The Beginning of Chinese Characters

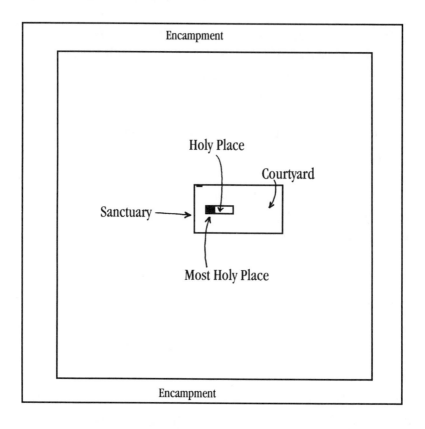

When the Israelites left Egyptian bondage under the leadership of Moses, it was following ten devastating plagues sent by God to impress upon the cruel ruling Egyptian pharaoh to let the Israelites leave Egypt. The plagues were also to show that God was the universal Ruler and that the Israelites were to be His chosen people and to be His witnesses on earth. God led these people through the wilderness by His Presence in a cloud by day and a fiery pillar at night. When the cloud moved, the vast multitude was to move also. When it stopped, they were to pitch camp. They had been led to a large open space before Mount Sinai. Here they camped for over a year to hear the instructions of their divine Leader through Moses.

The sanctuary was to be God's focus to teach them many forgotten attributes of God. During their centuries of slavery in Egypt, the Israelites had

Appendix II—Significance of the Sanctuary

been unable to sacrifice animals, that looked forward to a coming Savior, as the first couple had been taught initially when expelled from their garden home in Eden. Sinners were once more to learn of God's mercy and forgiveness when they sacrificed a lamb, representing the Savior to come. God specified all of the sanctuary services.

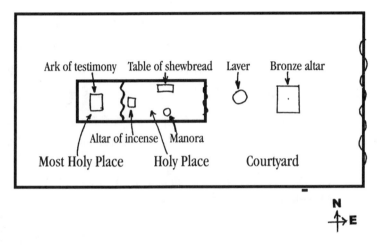

A sinner must enter the courtyard of the sanctuary with his lamb. The boundaries of the courtyard were white linen sheets, that formed an enclosing wall. The courtyard symbolically represented the earth where the sinner himself took the life of the lamb, even as Adam sacrificed an animal before the closed gate of Eden. Outside the sanctuary, in the courtyard, was a bronze "horned" altar. At the corners of the altar hearth were four horns upon which the officiating priest put blood from the sacrificed animal. The sacrifice was also burned upon this altar, even as *"[Jesus} that He might sanctify the people with His own blood, suffered outside the gate. (Hebrews 12: 12)*. Between the altar and the sanctuary was a basin-laver where the priests could wash their hands and feet before entering the tabernacle.

Only the priests entered the sanctuary. In the Holy Place were three items of furniture, each symbolizing an attribute of the Savior to come. On the north side of this larger apartment was the table of shewbread with 12 loaves of bread—one for each of the 12 tribes of Israel. Jesus Christ would later explain, *"I am the bread of life." (John 6: 48)*. He was man's Sustainer. On the south side of this first apartment was a seven-branched candlestick [manora] with ever-burning flames. Again, Jesus would explain, *"I am the light of the world." (John 8: 12)* He is the divine Director.

Before the elaborately embroidered curtain that divided the two apartments stood the golden "horned" altar of incense with ever-burning perfumed incense, representing Christ's continual intercession as man's Mediator. The veil itself symbolized Christ, for at the time of His crucifixion and death, *"behold, the veil of the temple was torn in two from top to bottom," (Matthew 27: 50, 51)*. Behind the curtain, the tables of stone, on which God Himself had inscribed the ten commandments, were stored in a golden chest in this Most Holy Place of the sanctuary. On the upper surface of the golden Ark, the "mercy seat," stood two golden angels [cherubim], facing toward each other with outstretched wings touching above the "Shekinah" glory of God's presence. This "Ark of the testimony" [containing God's law], with its "mercy seat," represented God's throne. Only the high priest, again representing Christ, could enter the Most Holy Place and come into God's very presence.

The parallel schemes of the earthly sanctuary and God's eternal dwelling place, the heavenly New Jerusalem, become apparent. The pattern for the earthly sanctuary, given by God Himself, can be traced to the heavenly. The Most Holy Place was the earthly dwelling place of God, His presence being manifested by the Shekinah glory. Both the sanctuary's Most Holy Place and the New Jerusalem have corresponding measurements: equal length, width and height. By understanding the services of the sanctuary and its design, God intended that man might have a glimpse of eternal truths. He designed the sanctuary and its services specifically so that man might understand that only the blood of the coming Savior, Jesus Christ, would ultimately bring salvation.

BIBLIOGRAPHY

A Collection of 22 Classic Writers (Shanghai: Classics Publication, 1996).
Chung-kuo k'e-hsueh-yuan K'ao-ku yen-chiu-so, *Chia-Ku Wen-Pien* (Peking: K'ao-ku-hsueh chuan-k'an yi-chung ti-shih-ssu hao, 1965
Chin Hsiang-cheng, *Hsu Chia-Ku Wen Pien* (Taipei: I Wen Yin Shu Kuan, 1959).
Chou Fa Kao, et al., *Ching Wen Ku Lin* (Hong Kong: Chinese University, 1975).
Chiyuan, *Etiology of Chinese Characters* (Beijing: The Commercial Press, 1979).
Chung-kuo K'e-hsueh-yuan k'ao-ku yen-chiu-so, *Chia-Ku Wen-Pien* (Peking: K'ao-ku hsueh chuan-k'an yi chung ti-shih-ssu hao, 1965).
Durant, Will, *The Story of Civilization: Our Oriental Heritage, Babylonia* (New York: Simon and Schuster, 1941).
Faber, George Stanley, *The Origin of Pagan Idolatry* (London: R. & C. Rivingtons, 1816).
Gia Fu Feng and English, Jane, *Translation of Lao Zi, Tao Te Ching* (Toronto: Vintage Books, Random House, Inc., 1989).
Hall, Edward, *The Wall Chart of World History* (London, Dorset Press, 1988).
Hawley,, W.M,, *Oriental Culture Chart # 6* (Chinese Seal Characters)
Hung Pei Chiang, *Ching Wen P'ien Wen* (Taipei: Kung I Publ. Co., 1974.)
Hung Pei Chaing, *Chih Ku Lu Chuan Wen, Vol II* (Taipei: Lo Pien Publ. Co., 1974).
Iia Gu Wen, *Zi Shuo Li* (Taiwan: An Guo Jun, 1993)
Kang Xi Dictionary (Taipei: Da Shem Publ., 1978)
Karlgren, Bernhard, *Grammata Seroca* (Taipei: Ch'eng wen Publ. Co., 1966).
Legge, James, *The Notions of the Chinese Concerning God and Spirits*

(Hong Kong : Hong Kong Register Office, 1852).
Legge, James, *The Chinese Classics, Vol. III, The Shu Jing* (Taipei: SMC Publ. Inc., 1983).
Lin Chih Ch'ing, *Ting Cheng Liu Shu T'ung* (Shanghai: Kuang I Publ. Co., 1936).
Lung Ch'uan Kuei T'ai Lang, *Shih Chi Hui Chu K'ao Cheng* (Taipei: Han Ching wen Hua Enterprise Co., Ltd., 1983).
MacDonald, Malcolm, *Angkor* (London: Jonathan Cape, 30 Bedford Square, 1958).
Mathews, R. H., *Mathews' Chinese-English Dictionary* (Cambridge, Mass: Harvard University Press, 1975, revised).
Ma Wei Ching, *Wei Ching Chia Ku Wen Yuan* (Yunlin: Ma Fu Distributor, 1971).
Nelson, Ethel R., Broadberry, Richard, and Chock, Ginger, *God's Promise to the Chinese* ((Dunlap, TN: Read Books Publ., 1997).
Smith, William, *Dictionary of the Bible* (Hartford: J.B. Burr & Co., 1868).
The Horizon Book of Lost Worlds (New York: American Heritage Publ. Co., 1962).
Wang, Samuel and Nelson, Ethel R., *God and the Ancient Chinese* (Dunlap, TN: Read Books Publisher, 1998).
Wei Zhengtong, *The Wisdom of China* (Taipei: The Cowboy Publishing Co., Ltd., 1977).
Wilder, G.D. and Ingram, J.H. *Analysis of Chinese Characters*, (Taipei: Chin Wen Publ. Co., 1964).
Wu Shuping, Lai Chang-yang, *The Four Books and five Jing in Modern Chinese* (Beijing: International Culture Publication, Inc., 1996).
Xi-pao Mei *The Works of Mo Zi* (China: Confucius Publishing Co.)

NOTE; Definitions are those found in *Mathews' Chinese-English Dictionary* that most nearly correspond to the original oracle bone or bronzeware pictograms. Additional definitions are listed under each radical in the main text.

RADICAL INDEX

Radical	Traditional	Oracle Bone	Bronzeware	Page
1 One	一	¥		25
2				
3 flame of fire	丶	◇	●	23
4 (breath)	ノ	(*Shuo Wen*)	⌒	40
5 second	乙	∫	∫	46
6				
7 two, above	二	=	=	198
8 above, cover	亠			215
9 man, person	人	⟨	⟨	67
10 man, person	儿	⟨	⟨	67
11 to enter	入	入		78

253

Radical	Traditional	Oracle Bone	Bronzeware	Page
12				
13 a border	冂			216
14 cover (hill)	冖	∩		114
15				
16				
17 receptacle	凵	∪		208
18 knife	刀	⌇		169
19 strength	力	⌇	⌇	49
20 enfold, wrap	勹	⌇		104
21 spoon (person)	匕		∧	49
22 box	匚	⊏	⊟	175
23 hide	匸			175
24 perfect	十	∣	◆	25
25 to divine	卜	⊦		45

Radical Index

Radical	Traditional	Oracle Bone	Bronzeware	Page
26 command				81
27 hill, cliff				108
28 certain person				147
29 also, ans				34
30 mouth, person				21
31 enclosure				170
32 earth, soil				68
33 mature male				69
34 to follow				113
35				
36 dusk				76
37 great (man)				66
38 woman				79
39 son, offspring				71

The Beginning of Chinese Characters

Radical	Traditional	Oracle Bone	Bronzeware	Page
40 roof	宀		∩	95
41				
42 little, humble	小	ᛌ	⁂	26
43				
44 repres. of dea	尸	⟩		143
45 beginning, plants	屮	ψ	Y	59
46 mountain, island	山	⩗	▲▲▲	106
47 river	川	⦙	⦚⦚⦚	193
48 to work	工	工		70
49 self	己	乙		145
50 covering	巾			176
51 shield	干	甾	Y	195
52 small	幺	8	8	82
53 roof	广	∩		122

Radical Index

Radical	Traditional	Oracle Bone	Bronzeware	Page
54 long walk	夂	介		208
55 hands joined	廾	🖐	🖐	115
56 dart	弋			44
57 curved	弓			144
58				
59 (God's presence)	彡	(Shuo Wen 彡)		37
60 small step	彳			207
61 heart	心			109
62 weapon	戈			166
63 door	戶			167
64 hand	扌			114
65 a branch	支			46
66 to rap, ("Helper")	攴			47
67 elegant	文			44

The Beginning of Chinese Characters

Radical	Traditional	Oracle Bone	Bronzeware	Page
68				
69				
70 central, square	方	丼	方	189
71				
72 sun	日	☉	☉	74
73 to speak	曰	ㅂ	曰	40
74 moon	月	☽		76
75 tree	木	朩	朩	136
76 short of	欠	𠂆		204
77 stop, rest	止	㐃		206
78 vicious	歹	冎		162
79 to kill	殳		殳	48
80 not, forbid	毋	毋		146
81 compare	比	𠤎		80

258

Radical Index

Radical	Traditional	Oracle Bone	Bronzeware	Page
82 hair	毛			217
83 family;, clan	氏			68
84 breath	气			36
85 water	水			192
86 fire	火			220
87 hand (of God)	爪			24
88 Father	父			32
89 communicate	爻			123
90				
91				
92 tooth, serrated	牙			210
93 bullock	牛			169
94 dog	犬			*64*
95				

259

The Beginning of Chinese Characters

Radical	Traditional	Oracle Bone	Bronzeware	Page
96 gem, valuable	玉	王		93
97				
98 earthen pottery	瓦	∂		86
99 sweet	甘	⊌		121
100 bring forth life	生	ψ		58
101 use, purpose	用	甶		33
102 garden, field	田	田	田	104
103 foot	疋	♂		160
104				
105 back-to-back	癶	ᖮ (*Shuo Wen* ᗜᗝ)		124
106 white, pure	白	θ	⊻	195
107				
108 vessel	皿	⊻	⊻	88
109 eye	目	▱	⌀	118

Radical Index

Radical	Traditional	Oracle Bone	Bronzeware	Page
110				
111 arrow	矢			42
112 rock	石			191
113 to manifest	示			27
114				
115 growing grain	禾			111
116				
117 stand up, create	立			70
118 bamboo	竹			60
119 rice, grain	米			60
120 delicate, fine	糸			149
121 earthenware	缶			84
122				
123 sheep	羊			174
124 wings	羽			116

The Beginning of Chinese Characters

Radical	Traditional	Oracle Bone	Bronzeware	Page
125 venerable	老			218
126				
127				
128 ear	耳			123
129 command	聿			137
130 flesh	肉			77
131 statesman	臣			119
132 origin	自			139
133 arrive at	至			43
134 hold in hands	臼	(Seal:)		92
135 tongue	舌			32
136				
137 vessel	舟			90
138				

Radical Index

Radical	Traditional	Oracle Bone	Bronzeware	Page
139				
140 grass	艹	↓↓	↓↓	59
141 tiger	虍			63
142 reptile	虫			158
143 blood	血			172
144 crossroad, walk	行			200
145 clothes	衤			168
146 west	西			74
147 to visit	見			113
148 horn	角			196
149 word	言			30
150 valley	谷			209
151 bronze vessel	豆			88
152 pig	豕			64

The Beginning of Chinese Characters

Radical		Traditional	Oracle Bone	Bronzeware	Page
153	footless reptile	豸			140
154	precious	貝			138
155	naked, red	赤			83
156	to run	走			204
157	foot	足			158
158	body	身			157
159					
160	bitter, grievous	辛			29
161	early morning	辰			110
162	walking	辶			126
163	city	邑			212
164					
165	distinguished	采			140
166	sorrow	里			163

Radical Index

Radical		Traditional	Oracle Bone	Bronzeware	Page
167	gold, precious	金		全	94
168	old	長		㐨	220
169	gate	門	門		166
170	mount, hill	阝	𠃌	𠃎	109
171					
172	bird	隹	鳥		39
173	rain	雨	雨		35
174	produce	靑	㞢	㞢	93
175	wrong, not	非	非	非	137
176	face-to-face	面	面	面	117
177					
178	turn away	韋	韋	韋	162
179					
180	musical note	音	音	音	205

265

The Beginning of Chinese Characters

Radical	Traditional	Oracle Bone	Bronzeware	Page
181 the head	頁	ᑰ	ᑰ	118
182 wind, breath	風	凵	𩙿	38
183 go quickly	飛	(Seal: 飛	飛)	41
184 food	食	食		120
185 beginning, first	首	ᑰ	ᑰ	125
186 delicious	香	香		120
187 horse	馬	馬	馬	64
188 bone	骨	骨		78
189 high, lofty	高	高	高	216
190 hair	髟			218
191 fight	鬥	鬥		173
192				
193 large clay pot	鬲	鬲	鬲	85
194 alien, devil	鬼	鬼	鬼	164

Radical Index

Radical	Traditional	Oracle Bone	Bronzeware	Page
195 fish	魚			61
196 bird	鳥			62
197				
198 deer	鹿			64
199 wheat	麥			60
200 hemp	麻			61
201 yellow	黃			105
202 millet	黍			59
203 evil, black	黑			165
204				
205 toad, strive	黽			62
206 sacrificial vessel	鼎			86
207 stir up	鼓			89
208 rat	鼠			65

The Beginning of Chinese Characters

Radical	Traditional	Oracle Bone	Bronzeware	Page
209 first, before	鼻			87
210 all alike	齊			107
211 teeth, beginning	齒			211
212 dragon	龍			159
213 tortoise	龜			62
214 flute	龠			112

Radical	Simplified	Oracle Bone	Bronzeware	Page
(90) Heaven, God	天			22
(144) to produce	申			28
(168) inferior to	亞			199
(172) light, naked	光			83
(192) to restrain	束			148